Orphaned by Suicide

ALICIA SEWDASS RAMDHAREE

Orphaned by Suicide

life after losing an entire family to a murder-suicide

INSPIRED
PUBLISHING

Orphaned by Suicide
Life after losing an entire family to a murder-suicide
First Edition, First Impression 2021
ISBN: 978-1-77630-673-2
Copyright © Alicia Sewdass Ramdharee

Published by:
Inspired Publishing
PO Box 82058 | Southdale | 2135
Johannesburg, South Africa
Email: info@inspiredpublishing.co.za www.inspiredpublishing.co.za

The stories in this book reflect the author's recollection of events.
Some names, locations and identifying characteristics have been
changed to protect the privacy of those depicted. Dialogue has
been recreated from memory. Any similarity to actual persons,
living or dead, is purely coincidental.

I wish that; as a child someone would save me,
I wish that; as a child someone would save me from my mind,
I wish that; as a child someone had comforted me instead of calling
it a performance,
I wish that; as a child someone saw my raw, hurt heart,
I wish that; as a child someone saw how damaged I was after losing
my family,
I wish that; as a child someone saw that I had lost
-a mum
-a dad
-a brother
-a sister,
I wish that; as a child someone didn't blame me for my family's
murder-suicide,
I wish that; as a child someone took me into their arms and held me
close,
I wish that; as an Adult no other child or person suffers a murder-
suicide.

Alicia 'Sewdass' Ramdharee

In loving memory of:
Dad- Des Sewdass
Mum- Sunitha Sewdass
Sister- Tasha Sewdass
Brother- Shivenn Sewdass

My family lost their lives to a Murder- Suicide "11 December 99"

DEDICATION

I dedicate this book to the Warriors from my Suicide Awareness support group "Surviving Suicide".

To all Survivors, Victims and people that have lost loved ones to suicide.

To my family and friends that stood by me, thank you!

To my maternal family, thank you for taking me in, I know it was not an easy task for you, I am forever grateful that you kept me.

My dear husband, Schivan Ramdharee, I love you and thank you for being my pillar of strength and for always supporting my dreams.

Above all... my humble Pranams to my Guru "Sri Sathya Sai Baba". You've answered my prayers, given me strength, hope and blessings beyond my imagination. You loved me when no one else did, you blessed me without passing judgement, you always worked your miracles. Bless your divine Soul...

Om Sai Ram

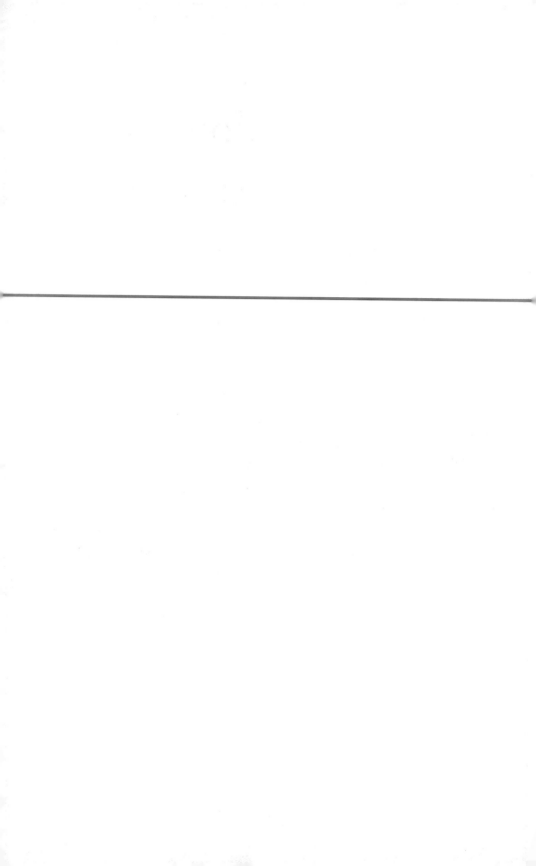

Table of Contents

PART 1   **11**

Suicide: The Silent Killer   13
The Beginning   21
Growing Up   26
The Wedding   45
Tragedy Strikes   60
Days to Come   81
Time to Move   100
Dating Game   114
Moving Again   120
School Life   138
Finding Love   150
Becoming Miss Independent   161

PART 2   **185**

New Beginnings   187
It's Not Over   214
Telling the World   241
Swami and His Divine Love   251

PART 3   **261**

Reflections   263
Crucial Conversations   276

SYNOPSIS

I was 12 years old when I lost my family to a violent murder-suicide. Life after this terrible ordeal was harsh and worst of all, I had to face the world without my beautiful family. The life of an orphan is a world of its own. I grew up in communities where there is a stigma that surrounds suicide and mental health. Something I wish we could be rid of. I was told not to speak of my Dad's murder-suicide, told to lie. I had to bear the brunt of my Dad's actions. I moved from home to home within my maternal family. My life was hard, not as easy as my bubbly personality reflects. As the years passed, I gained strength to live another day. Where I had dreamed of ending it all, contemplating suicide became a thing of the past for me as I looked forward to celebrating the life that I was left to lead. Marriage started a brand new chapter in my life, it was time for ME. Years later I felt a calling that it was time to share my story with the world. The *new me* took to social media, sharing my story on video with the hope of saving lives.

Soon after that, I began my Suicide Awareness support group. This group started to give hope, inspiration and motivation to the millions of Warriors out there. This book is an in-depth account of my life. Sharing my story was just the tip of the iceberg. I assure you there was deep pain. I wonder how I coped through it all. I wrote this book not for pity or fame, but to create awareness about suicide and mental health. Think twice before attempting suicide or anything that will inflict pain on you and the ones you love. I want the world to see it from my view, the view of an orphan.

PART 1

1

SUICIDE: THE SILENT KILLER

suicide noun

sui·cide | \ ˈsü-ə-ˌsīd \

DEFN: *death caused by injuring oneself with the intent to die.*

What a word!

A word that causes a huge impact on lives worldwide. Some claim that Suicide is the easy way out. I beg to differ. We never know what the next person is going through mentally, emotionally or physically. We live in such a judgmental world. I realized this not long after my family's death. There is a stigma that hangs around the victims, survivors and people lost to suicide. People are judged by their actions and feelings. Many have been called cowards or weak, among other names.

A lot of people suffer in silence because of our community's lack of showing support or help. Instead of helping, we choose to pass remarks and judge. We tell those who are suffering to water down the story or not mention anything, like in my case. We tend to keep family secrets hidden to uphold the image of the family, or we are told to maintain that unbreakable silence that cuts so deep, to avoid being mocked and shamed. So, when does it really STOP? When do people that are going through things talk about it?

How many times have we confided in friends and family, only to hear our stories making headlines in the latest gossip? I guess this is the reason so many people out there choose not to talk. So many of us feel superior compared to those around us, never knowing how much they are suffering in silence.

In my dad's situation, we never saw any signs of suicidal thoughts or a change in his behavior, it just happened. I have heard that many people don't show signs that they are planning suicide. Some will mention that they are or have been contemplating it. That should raise a warning that we need to offer a lending ear, listen without judgment and direct this person to seek help. It is most important that they have someone to talk to, someone that shows them that they matter in this lifetime. Let us not push this person away, mock and cause more pressure. My father's suicide happened without warning.

Silently!

The survivors of suicide are always left behind to pick up the pieces after a loved one's suicide. We are left with the daunting questions, the endless "Why's", the "What-ifs", the "I could haves". We beat ourselves up for not having the answers that nobody knows, except for the person that is no longer with us. I always say that suicide is a vicious cycle.

We become victims and survivors of suicide. I wish I could end this thing called suicide along with the stigma and challenges one faces.

I want this book to speak loud and clear to the world, to show them how my dad's suicide has affected my life and that suicide is not the way to go.

Suicide is never a SOLUTION! Suicide destroys. There are many programs, institutions, walk-in centers, professionals, support groups, helplines, and information available if you need help.

You are not alone.

I am writing this book to show you that I MADE IT, I AM HERE FOR YOU, I WILL FIGHT FOR YOU TO LIVE!

PLEASE CHOOSE LIFE, IT IS WORTH LIVING AND SEEING YOURSELF BLOOM!

I am just one of many who have lost their loved ones to suicide. My story is just a drop in the ocean and I hope the ripple effect changes the mindset of many. We are here to help. Please do not choose suicide, choose to live, choose to celebrate life!

We all go through tough times. It may seem as though the walls are closing in and there is no way out, but I promise you that somebody out there is vouching for you, someone out there is praying for you to be blessed and protected. Please do not give up. I used the following story in my Support Group as an example of not giving up. I love telling stories about nature especially when it's from my very own garden. I will share the piece with you below:

Story about my Clivia...

I bought this plant 6 years ago. According to the nursery, it was in the sick section and not for sale. But I purchased it anyway, for R10! With just one leaf to show I planted this beauty, hoping to bring her back to life and see her bloom.

It was a struggle, she did well then lost her leaves and her sister plants. I kept moving her from pot to ground and different areas in my garden. I never gave up on my Clivia plant. I did research to see what she likes.

Finally, she found her place in this big green pot under the trees. She was happy and started growing out and soon she had so many sister plants. Every year I waited patiently to see if she would bloom!

Clivias bloom around August/September, and all my other Clivias bloomed. All except for this beauty. I let her be. I knew when she was ready to show off her flowers she would. And then it happened! Early in the August of 2020, I spotted not one, but two stems with buds. Oh, the joy I felt in my heart!

These were her blooms I had waited for 6yrs!
How often do we give up on ourselves and the people we care about?
We expect change immediately!
We don't have patience!

When we are ready to bloom in the environment we are in, we will. Continue to shower yourself, and others, with love and care. The end results, no matter how long they take, are worth the wait. You too will flower; you too are beautiful even if you have only one leaf to show. There is someone out there watching you grow, cheering you on for every leaf grown, for every struggle won.

There is someone out there that doesn't want you to give up. You too can bloom. It may take time, but you WILL get there.

Photo: Clivia 09 September 2020
Location: Alicia Ramdharee's garden

In those early days, I deliberated my own suicide. The pain of living without them became too much for me to handle. Nobody gives you a manual on "How to live without" once a loved one passes.

Life was hard growing up without my parents and siblings at my side. I missed them dearly. Try imagining going through your teen, youth and adult years without your parents. You are truly blessed if you still have your parents and siblings around. There is not a day that goes by without me thinking of mine.

I've so often wondered what my life would have been like with my parents and siblings, had they still been alive. We often think we will not be missed, and the world will be a better a place after our suicide attempt, but there is a great sadness and longing that is left.

Nobody can replace YOU!

I had to come to the realization that this life is my reality. I must live it to the fullest. What I thought would break me, made me stronger! Suicide took away my family, it robbed me of my happiness and time that I will never get back, but after you read this book, you will understand why I am the way I am.

You will understand why I have made certain decisions about how I live my life. I live my life as I see fit, based on reality and I don't do things "Just because".

A lot of people will disagree about what I have mentioned in this book. I know that I will get backlash from this. I want to say that it is okay. Everyone has their own views and everyone has viewed my life differently. However, this is my view and how I was left alone in this world, to live a life without my family. I ask that you remain respectful of my reality, as I remain respectful of yours.

To the many Warriors out there…

I hope my story inspires you to keep living. I hope this book makes you understand, see things through a different view and see it through the eyes of an orphan.

REFLECTION

Look deeper, take note, sometimes eyes scream for help and we just brush it off. We need to be aware. It's those silent screams that are the loudest. Walk in their shoes for a minute, it's not all roses and straight paths. We are stronger than we think!

2

THE BEGINNING

I am not very clued up with how things were before my arrival, but let me share with you what I have been able to piece together.

My Dad Des Sewdass, lived on a sugar-cane farm in Stanger, on the South Coast of Kwa-Zulu Natal, with his mum, dad, brothers and sisters. They were not very well- off, but they made it living day-to-day. He was born in August 1959, and was tall, healthy and dark in complexion. He always wore glasses. He became a teacher, amongst many other things. My dad was a "jack of all trades". I had the privilege of meeting my paternal grandparents. My grandfather, who I called Arja, which means paternal grandfather and my grandmother, Arji, which means paternal grandmother. They were very humble people and had a lot of knowledge which I wish I had grasped. My Arja was like a wizard. He knew all the Mantras (prayer recitals) for any prayer or sickness. He was bandy legged, his legs always bent in opposite directions, a bit dark in complexion, he never liked wearing shoes, always wore a toppie (a gentlemen's hat), shorts, shirt and used a walking stick. He had these deep dark brown eyes. My Arji had the most beautiful green eyes and lovely long hair which was always in a plait and oiled with coconut oil. Arji was always dressed in a Sari (a 6-9 meter cloth that is draped on a lady's body). I remember that every time she laughed, her whole tummy would shake. She was fair skinned. Both my grandparents spoke in Hindi with a bit of English. My dad's parents used to grow their own vegetables and make their own snuff/quai (made out of dry aloe leaves also known as shlaba).

My Mum, Sunitha Palad Maharaj, was born in January 1967, and lived in Mariannhill, with her mum, dad, brother and sisters. There were also many other family members that stayed not far off, on the hills. They lived in tin houses that were painted blue. They were given the names "The blue house" or "Tin house". My mum was short, fair in complexion, and had a model's figure. She was always well dressed. In short, my mum was gorgeous. As far as I know, she was a housewife. I don't remember her working.

I also had the great pleasure of meeting her parents. My maternal grandfather, who I called Nana, and my maternal grandmother, Nani, or as we all ended up calling her, "Ma". My Nana was dark in complexion, with hazel, honey-colored eyes. He was thin and a medium height. He was a top athlete back in his day. They also worked on the farms or bought vegetables from the local farmers and sold them to their customers. He was always well dressed and loved his cigarettes and beer. My Nani was a very fair-skinned woman. She had long hair, always dressed up nicely, in more skirts and dresses and she was slim and short. She worked from time to time and at other times, she was a housewife.

Truth be told, I was way too young to remember any vivid details, so this chapter is only based on what I can remember. Please bear with me because old age has definitely caught up with me.

We had the best of both worlds. As far as I can remember, both my grandmothers were the best cooks. I loved and always looked forward to, any meal prepared by either of them. I was not short of love from either side of my grandparents.

Well, as you know, at a certain age we have to start lives and families of our own. And my parents took that decision. I am not sure how my parents love story started, but they met and married on, 6 July 1985, happy or not, but married. If you do the math, my mum was 18 years old and my dad 26 years old, 8 years my mums senior.

From what I saw in their photos and from studying their body language, both my parents seemed very happy. Yes, I know photos do lie, but this is all I have. Good, happy and beautiful memories. I have to mention that my Mum was actually like a Princess from a fairy tale because my Mum had the most beautiful long hair. Wow! I had my very own Rapunzel! So the life of these two individuals began as one.

Let's fast-track to the year 1987. Why, you may ask? Because that is when the greatest most "*awesome*" person was born… ME! Alicia Sewdass! My parents had found out that they were expecting. A little girl who would enter the world somewhere in August.

Oh, how happy the Sewdass and Maharaj families were. They would soon have a grandchild in the family, small feet running around, pulling things down, crying, laughing, what a joyous occasion.

My mum carried well for the 9 months. I am unsure of all of her cravings but I am sure they were all good.

23

I'd like to think back on how excited both my parents were. Or to relive their excitement. I am sure it must be a big deal for first time parents. The excitement between them must have been overwhelming. All I can picture in my head is mum and dad anxiously waiting to meet me, a little girl waiting to grace them with her presence.

Mum's thoughts probably raced on endlessly.
What would she name her baby girl?
What should she dress her baby in?

My dad was probably thinking of all the fun the two of them would have once the baby was born. How fantastic that it was another August baby. I'm sure nobody could contain their excitement. Every month mum went for her appointments religiously.

As the months went by, they both watched how little me grew in mum's tummy. The two people who created me had become my mum and dad. I would be lying if I say I remember being yanked out and slapped on the butt, and the first look of my parents as well as the first taste of breast milk.

Legend goes that the first glance of a baby's parents is an imprint on their souls. The day a parent is assigned to a child, that parent becomes God for the child. These two people became my everything and I, theirs.

REFLECTION

Our forefathers, grandparents and parents are the reason why we are all here today. The cycle of Life. Giving life and living for the generations to come. There is a reason for every person born. With every life brought into this world there is a purpose. Your life matters.

3

GROWING UP

So, the days moved on. Filled with the changing of toweling nappies (yes, I said toweling nappies) remember, this was 1987. There was no such thing as disposable diapers yet. These were washed daily, and boy, did I soil them! Sorry mum, but I couldn't hold it back.

Shame, my mum had to hand wash all of those.

Oh, the joys of motherhood. I guess it comes with the package. From what I have gathered from my Mosi's, (Mother's sisters, i.e my aunts) I had colic, so I troubled my parents a lot in the early days. Time flew by though, and soon I was crawling, walking, teething, pulling things off the tables I could reach. I got to taste real food and started cooking lessons by doing the basics: "playing with pots and pans". And I was daddy's little girl. My daddy spoilt me so much. Photos were taken for every birthday. Birthdays were always a special occasion in my home. Dad would always put up décor and mum would lay out the table with eats and cakes. Yummy! I was dad's tomboy. I fixed cars, went fishing and did a lot with dad. I remember mum always loved dressing me up in very lady-like dresses, long white stockings, or lace socks. I have a few pictures in my album, not something I would want to wear now, but I guess back then it was fashion. My mum always dressed me up well.

There comes a time when all the fun must stop and reality takes control. As I got older, mum taught me a lot. Not knowing that my mum was preparing me for pre-primary school. I felt sorry for myself because this time saw the end of those comfy, late mornings and late nights. I was growing up and I had to face all that had to come my way (remember this line). Finally, the DAY had arrived. I was 5-6 years old and ready for pre-school. I was so excited or... not really. I guess I had mixed emotions, I was excited but also scared. My memories of pre-primary school are very vague, but I will try to recall them.

In my child-like brain, starting school, having to go to a strange, new place and having early morning wake-up calls seemed like a nightmare. Thankfully, I had a cousin who was starting school with me. It made things easier. She had a strong mindset and I really looked up to her.

Eventually the day arrived, and it was time for this little ray of sunshine to leave the burrow. I would resist being woken up so early, and dad would have to carry me out of bed. I couldn't understand why this was happening. Why did I need to go to school? Despite my protests, mum would wash me up and begin to dress me. I gave my parents grief for dressing me up every morning. I hated wearing socks. Do you know that line on the inside of the sock? Yes, well that line caused a lot of tantrums just because I could feel it on my toes. Who knew there was so much irritation built up inside of me? There were crocodile tears every morning because of this. But wait, that's not all I cried for! I had a brown school bag, it looked almost like a suitcase, with a flip clip. Dad wrote my name on the inside just in case I misplaced it. And that was done with basically everything, pencils, crayons, lunch boxes, clothing and juice bottles. On the first day, if I remember correctly, my mum's youngest sister came to stay with us. The idea was that she would take me to school, if mum was there, I would cry.

My motto for that day was: "I WON'T CRY". Man, did I fool myself. At school, we stood in lines waiting for, I don't know what. At that age, if I stood in a line, it was either to pay for groceries or to get free food. This was not the case and then, from what seemed like nowhere, BAM! I'm sitting in a class full of kids, crying their lungs out. I looked around to find a familiar face and then I realized I was alone in this room filled with crying kids and an aunty (the teacher) I didn't know.

I wanted my mummy to take me home, I did not want to be there. I wanted my mum's sister. Tears just came tumbling out of those eyes. What a long day without my mum. A day without my mum felt like forever and the feeling was terrible.

What a horrible day. If this day felt so bad without my mum, wait until we go deeper into my life. Imagine a life without parents or siblings for now.

I thought it would go better as the days went on. I was now a master of going to school. Since dad was a teacher, he left early to travel to Chatsworth. That is where he taught, so he could not take me to school. Mum did not have a license so she could not take me to my Primary school. The school that I attended was the same one that my entire family had gone to. My grandparents, mother, aunts, and uncles had all gone there. Due to the transport issue, we found a lady who transported kids to and from school. We called her the "transport Aunty", though her real name was Aunty Mala. She drove a red van with a canopy. This aunty and my mum arranged that I travel with her. I would kick up a storm in the morning. I had to wake up early, bath or just change, brush my teeth, then if I had to put on socks, you can just imagine the drama. My socks had to fit perfectly on my feet. If I felt one thing was off, or it hurt my toes, I would pull them off. Yes, this was done with a tantrum and a few smacks from mum. The same went with the dress and jersey. It just irritated the daylights out of me. They were either to pokey, too tight, or the tag annoyed me. I was such a drama queen.

Anyway, I would have my breakfast then wait outside for the transport lady. I had to memorize my home address and telephone number just in case I got lost. To date, I still remember my address and my house telephone number. They have been permanently engraved in my head.

So, there I would be. All dressed for school. I had a lot of rotten teeth. Kids my age had a fashion statement to up hold. You had to have rotten teeth. The transport lady would arrive and I would jump on the back of her van. We would get to school, and everyone would jump out. Everyone except me. I would stay plastered to the back and refuse to jump off. I would cry for my mummy.

Eventually, the transport lady would take me home. This went on for a while until one day the transport lady took me crying, to my class. I spent the whole day at school. I guess I got used to it, after that. I stopped resisting for a while, then started again during school hours. I would run to one of the classrooms where my neighbor attended classes. I would sit next to her until the school day had finished. School was just so scary for me, but when I got used to this new environment, I did stop crying in the mornings, and I finally got the hang of school. Later, I made friends and moved on with my kiddie days, playing and carefree.

One vivid memory I have of school was that we would go to the paddock. There, we had a jungle gym, a sand pit, swings and so much more. One day, we all stood in a line and I remember wearing my Bubble Gummers shoe and I really needed to Pee, but I was too scared to ask the teacher and I pee'd in my pants. My shoes were all messed up. Some days were really nice and some days were horrid. Soon it was time for holidays and I was back home, safe and sound in my mummy's arms.

After pre-school, it was class one, and the learning of mathematics and spelling tests came into practice. Making new friends and trying to be part of a group in school was hard work. I had a cousin in the same class, so we hung out. I loved being classroom monitor, writing on the chalkboard and my lunch breaks were always fun.

My school was so big, I was so afraid of the grounds and the steps that led us there. They seemed so huge for my tiny body. I told my parents that I could not go up and down the stairs and that they scared me. My superhero parents got into the car, drove me to school and walked up and down the stairs alongside me, to get me over my fear. I took a step, then hopped onto the next one. I wanted to walk like a normal kid down those stairs. Left leg then the right leg on the next step, and I wanted to go down and up quickly. Practice did make perfect though. I was so happy I had accomplished those big, mean stairs… with my parents' help, of course.

We had sports days too. We were placed in sports houses that were color coordinated. The colors were green and white (Lily), red and white (Carnation), yellow and black (Marigold), blue and white (Aster).

I was in the yellow house and we were well known for winning. It was always such a big event. We would get cream doughnuts and a juice in the morning before we started. Then we would have a parade around the grounds. My mummy was always at my sports days, and I always took part in athletics. Even though I was a hopeless athlete, Mum was always there to cheer me on. School was not all that bad.

Time flew by and I had a baby sister on the way. Tasha Sewdass was born in July 1991. She looked like a doll, such unique features, and the loveliest brown eyes. I was the proud big sister. I helped with what I could and babysat.

4 years later, we were blessed with another addition. A baby boy, Shivenn Sewdass, was born in the December of 1995. He was a miracle baby. We had thought we lost him. On one of my mums' appointments the doctor picked up that his heartbeat was very faint. Mum was rushed in for an emergency C-Section because the umbilical cord was wrapped around his neck.

He had glassy, black eyes, and pin straight hair. My brother was so majestic. I had the most adorable family but never looked after what I had. I used to get irritated with my brother and sister a lot. We fought the usual sibling arguments. I never tried to understand what went on in their minds, and what bugged me the most about them. We had some fun times though. We would wear our school uniform, (which was a white dress) walk outside and act like we were working in a LAB, dissecting aliens from "outer-space". This idea came from watching a TV series called the X-files, with mum and dad's supervision of course.

My sister and I once sprayed furniture polish on the floor and slid on it just to have fun, slipping and sliding. As much as we laughed, we cried when mum gave us a hiding for dirtying our white socks. We all loved spending time together in the garden, going out and having fun. That was our family time. On weekends, we three anxiously awaited the cartoons of "Tom and Jerry" or "Looney Toons". Back then we had to wait for "M-Net open time". It was a time of the day when you could watch special programs on M-Net. We would wait until the specific songs played, and as soon as open time started, we would be able to watch our cartoons.

I thought this was the life. We all had our ups and downs, but we loved each other a lot as a family. I say this like I knew exactly about ups and downs! Not really, but in my child-like brain, that's what I thought of as "my problems", only to find out later in life that there are far more serious problems then this!

I had changed schools when I was about to enter Standard 2, now known as Grade 4. There was a primary school across from where my dad taught. This would work out perfectly as we were planning to move to Chatsworth. I was sad to leave my friends but excited to make new ones.

My schooling years were fun. I enjoyed my primary school days a lot. I had more than enough friends, but you did get one or two that thought they were one better than you. They seemed to walk around with their noses in the air. All-in-all, though, it was great to have a lot of friends in my new school.

One rainy day, as I was walking in the corridor, a bully girl shoved me around and pushed me. I fell onto the muddy ground and my white dress was soiled. I cried and went to my dad. He was an art teacher, and his classes were always held in the library. I ran over to the school he taught in and one of the home economics teachers washed my school dress and we sat at the oven warming me up and drying my dress. Dad sent a message to my teachers to let them know about what had happened and that I would return to class as soon as I had dried my clothing. I can't remember what happened to that girl though. I was very thin and I think I was just always a target for a bully.

Standard 5 (Grade 7) was just my best primary school year. We were elected as prefects, and I enjoyed it because we got to have our way. We had to look after classes when the teachers where in meetings. I don't think I was the most popular girl to be with in school, but I had my friends there. I'm still thankful to those guys and girls.

I loved playing Netball in school. That's one sport I would love to play again. I was an ordinary student, but my parents were always there to support me in my studies, no matter what. When it was time to study, dad would wake me up early in the morning.

The night before, mum or dad would make me study a certain chapter and then he would test me on whatever I had studied. If I got one question wrong, I would get a hiding with whatever was in front of him. I was always petrified of my dad, especially when he got angry. He would make me cry until I knew my work. I guess that's why I did so well in school. I was lazy when it came to learning speeches by heart though. Remembering line for line was exhausting.

Mum always came to my rescue with her amazing baked goods to cheer me up. My mum was a pro at baking and cooking. I was very fond of her banana loaf and jam tarts. Dad was a good cook as well, waving that spoon of amazing biryani's and our weekend special - freshly baked scones.

We were disciplined for bad behavior. In those days, there was no such thing as not being allowed to discipline a child. I am glad I had that in school and at home. We respected our teachers, and we were petrified of them, especially if you didn't know your work. You'd be asking for the cane on an open palm or a twist of the ear. These days, it seems like the students don't respect their teachers, which is truly sad, and parents aren't allowed to discipline their children either. I feel there is a huge difference between abuse and discipline! I guess each to their own, but I am glad I grew up in an era where discipline and prayer were still present in school and at home.

I had to become a responsible child when my sister started her 1st year at pre-school, I felt so proud to have one of my siblings in the same school as me, and I never allowed anyone to hurt my sister. I stood by her at all times. There was a time when I needed to fetch her from school. Tasha was to wait for me at our usual waiting spot, but when I got there, she was not there. I waited a while and no one pitched up, so thinking she went home, I left. When I reached home, I asked mum if Tasha was at home. Mum said "NO" …

I felt like the world was going to crumble. I ran back to school and checked all over, classroom to classroom! My sister was nowhere to be seen. I went to my dad's school. (you just cross over a fence and you were in the High School) I asked dad where Tasha was and his reply was, that he didn't know. I was now in tears.

I ran back to school and checked again. She was still nowhere to be seen. I went back to dad, now scared, ready to report that I had could not find my sister. As I blurted it out, little madam walks out from the computer room, she'd been sitting there all this time! "Tasha!!!" I yelled out. "Have you any idea how worried I've been?" All she did was laugh. That was when I realized that I never wanted to lose either of my siblings. They were far too precious to me. What a day!!! I am sure you would go crazy as well.

My brother loved to play our house games and tea parties with us. We laughed, cried, sang and had tons of fun, just us three, in our little imaginary worlds.

We played hide and seek one day and I hid in my parent's cupboard. When he came along, I stayed in the cupboard and made scary noises and he got so scared, he ran and screamed. I couldn't help but laugh myself sick!!! It was funny.

In my heart, even though I used to get irritated with my siblings, I still loved them a lot. I remember the one day I hit my sister so hard on her back that she couldn't breathe. Tasha suffered a lot with asthma. We needed to use inhalers regularly, to help her when she had an attack. My parents tried reward charts on the wall, to motivate us not to fight. I guess that was one way they tried to help us get along. I had a wheezing issue from time to time, so I had an inhaler as well. My eczema became terrible in summer. It would ooze it looked so disgusting. One day, Dad took some methylated spirits and dabbed it on a piece of cotton wool. He applied it on all my eczema patches. It was on my leg, just below my knee, my elbows and on my bum. My eczema was oozing so much and all the ointments we had been given over the months never helped. To say it *stung* on those patches of skin would be a huge understatement! But it worked! It dried up and that was the last we had to deal with it. I have a beautiful scar on my leg from it, I was always embarrassed showing off my legs as I got older, but hey, scars have stories too, right? I have learnt to embrace my scar. I show off my scars and wear them proudly now.

My parents never abused us. I mentioned we were disciplined though. Some memories are: if you broke any plants you get hit on the hand", "no touching", if we didn't listen to an instruction we got locked in the bathroom until the tantrums stopped, you got chilies rubbed in your mouth for swearing or back chatting. Later on- we had the wooden spoon, hanger or the belt. The swearing bit never stopped with me, I started swearing in Grade 7. It got worse in high school and it just stuck. I know people say it's not lady like to swear, that it stains my beautiful personality.

A meme I read on a Facebook comment recently said: "People who swear are weak and have a lot to hide." Some say it's a defense mechanism. Whatever it is, I still swear and it's none of the above.

The people that know me well enough know that if we are chatting and I haven't sworn, something must be wrong. I DO NOT swear in front of elders in the family as I understand the need to maintain that respect. It's difficult because it is so ingrained as a part of my vocabulary. I am famous for my Gordon Ramsey style of speaking. I love Gordon Ramsey. He is just so awesome and straight forward. If you are reading this, Gordon Ramsey, you are F*****g awesome and I hope to meet you some day.

But back to the story! I enjoyed it when mum made me lay down on her lap and she would run her long nails through my hair. I loved it and would eventually fall off to sleep. Mum loved collecting perfumes. She always smelled so good.

I had the most precious gifts but had no clue what was in store for me for the rest of my life. I always wanted to see my parents grow old and I assumed I would end up looking after them. Getting my brother and sister to a higher level of studies and see them get married.

Wow, I had a huge dream and I just couldn't wait to see that day. Mum and Dad, as I have mentioned, disciplined us as any parent would. And when we were disciplined, I often contemplated how lucky orphans are because they didn't have parents to punish them.

I really wish I hadn't thought of how lucky orphans are! Because being one is not something nice.

On weekends, to make extra money, my dad would decorate stages and we would go to the flea markets to sell these hand painted polystyrene cartoon characters along with many other creative pieces that dad made. The little money that dad made from his sales helped a lot. Dad did a lot of signage for windows and posters for our local store in Mariannhill. Dad was strict and we girls were not allowed to use makeup or wear short dresses, not even to stay over alone at a friend or family's home. Dad always said "there is a time, place and age for things", and that is something I still truly believe in. When we went shopping as a family, we couldn't afford to purchase expensive things. The Rule: look at the price. If you feel it is too expensive and dad can't purchase it, leave it. In short, suit your pocket. There was one time-my birthday was coming up and I was allowed to choose clothing. I found a really lovely pair of cargo pants, but the price was too high. I showed dad and he promised, like always, "When I have money, I will buy them for you." And that is what he did. When he had enough money to spoil me, my dad purchased the pants. And I grew up with that throughout my life. We bought our clothes for R10, R20 from these factory shops. There were a few times I know of, that we purchased clothing for some of my cousins and they were not allowed to wear them because their mum said, "My children don't wear cheap clothes!"

Well, to me it was the thought that counts.

It was the same with Barbie dolls. We always played with these fake Barbie dolls. Their heads and arms would come off. Our cousins always got these cool "better, original toys" and we were always laughed at because we had cheap things. Dad made it his duty to buy us real Barbie dolls and so we finally got the real deal.

I loved my Dad and Mum a lot. I wish I had more time with them. My parents gave us the best and we appreciated all that they gave us. It may not have been the original stuff but they made a plan to give us things that every other child had. I know it was hard for them, even though as a child, we don't understand these things. I knew that if we were told that we would get it another time it was because we couldn't afford it then.

We always ate at home, we actually never knew what it was to eat in the restaurants, as dad didn't believe in eating out. We had to save money and use it for things that were priority. Those morals and values taught to me at such a young age, is what stayed with me. It was engraved in my head and that is what I still believe in.

I had my first period when I was 12 years old. I think it was after my 12th birthday. It really didn't make sense to me as to what all the excitement was. At that age nothing ever made sense. Mum was overjoyed. The house-phone didn't stop ringing that day. My mum was very supportive and there was this sense of calmness around her. She always made you feel better in a split second. She was a lovely soul. That day she sat outside the bathroom door and gave me a step by step tutorial on how to put on a pad. The cramps were really bad. I remember mum cuddling me on the steps of our Chatsworth home. And from time to time Mum would ask if I was ok. My body was changing. I was aware of that because in school we had meetings for girls only with our female teachers. I knew exactly what was going on in my body and why all these changes were happening. I was grateful that I had shared such a sacred part of my life while my mummy was still around.

I admired my mum and her beauty, and I wished to grow up to be just like her in every way. My mum dressed up every day. She always had her hair and make-up done. She was so beautiful. Flawless beauty. I never found fault in my parents I hoped to be married and live happily as they did. You could see their love. Mum and Dad called each other "Love", I believe I would call them Love as well when I was a toddler. We always had this thing when either one of our parents would ask "How much do you love me?" you would open your arms as wide as you could and show them this much. We always said I love you to each other, we always left home with a hug and kiss. My mum would always giggle every time I hugged and kissed her goodbye before leaving for school. Mum, on an early morning, standing in her gown, waiting as we trekked off. Dad would leave the car to idle and, one by one we would say goodbye. I was always the last one to kiss mum and the tip of my nose would touch her skin. With that little giggle and beautiful smile, she would say "Your nose is cold!" and I would squeeze her. Mum's scent was just so subtle, it's a smell I would notice anywhere. My feet, fingers and nose are still always cold.

I remember mum would always have little surprises for us. To some it may never mean much but to me it was the most amazing gift to receive. Mum would pick roses and have them pressed into the directory. Those days the directories were mammoth sized and really heavy. Mum would place the roses in the middle of the book and, weeks later, we had an amazing, pressed rose. It cheered me up all the time. It was magical and made with love. I would be so fascinated at the pressed rose and the form it took.

Mummy made the best stews. The memory of the taste still lingers in my mouth to this day. Her baking also always found room in our tummies. Everything she made tasted amazing. My mum was beautiful inside and out. It was said that my mum didn't know how to cook when she got married. My dad purchased an Indian Delights cookbook for her so she could learn. I have the book with me. On the first page, my dad drew a dedication to my mum dated in 1988. It's as old as I am.

We always visited family on weekends, or went to the park for a picnic. We all loved working in the garden. Planting was our way to destress, and it was our bonding time as a family. During our school holidays, we always traveled to Johannesburg to spend time with my maternal family. It was a lot of fun. Dad always made sure he visited and kept family bonds close. I remember in December there was always a grand feast at Ma's house, with Watermelons, Litchis and ripe Mangoes. Next to Ma's house was a house shop and that Uncle always gave us free ice-lollies or ice-cream.

Our Johannesburg family visited as well. While in Durban, some stayed in our home and others chose to rather book into hotels. My mum's eldest sister always booked into the hotels on the beach front, and my siblings and I always got to stay with them there. It obviously took a lot of convincing when it came to asking Dad! Remember the rule: "We go as a family." Staying in a hotel was a very different experience because we never got to do that with my parents. It was considered a huge luxury!

Although, I do remember a holiday when we went to the Drakensburg. It was our first ever holiday just as a family and we spent it with our neighbors. I don't remember much except that it was cold.

When dad did stage decors on weekends, if we all could, we tagged along to help. There were times where I would feel embarrassed, especially if it was at a friend's home. At this present age I am proud of my dad for doing so much on the side to keep us afloat. I never understood it as a child. Now, as an adult, I fully understand why certain sacrifices had to be made.

I had an amazing childhood, amazing parents and siblings.
We didn't live off name brands, even though I wished I could be like the "cool kids" in my school. Simple Simon was the way.

I was not allowed to eat pork and beef. Due to our Hindu beliefs, it was totally against our house rules BUT I broke them. I broke them, not to prove a point or be disrespectful to my religion, I did it because I wanted to taste it and I liked it.

Mondays and Tuesdays were fasting days in our home. That meant no meat. Strictly vegetarian meals were prepared. My friend loved my vegetarian lunches and I loved her ham sandwiches- so we would swop without my parents knowing. Our childhood was short of nothing. There was a time Mum noticed I liked a boy of a family friend. He was my age, and a very handsome chap. I will never forget the conversation Mum and I had. It was brief and Mum obviously didn't tell Dad about me "liking a boy", he would have been furious. Mum's words, as I remember, were: "Don't chase after boys, there is a time for it, don't rush into marriage or get married young. Rather travel and see the world, my child."

Those words stuck with me and I treasured it. A mother's advice to her 12-year-old daughter. Was this a clue to something I had never seen? I don't know.

Maybe one day I would understand.

REFLECTION

As we start finding our way in this life, we learn, we develop personalities and habits. What may be seen as good for one is bad for the other and vice versa, regardless of it we learn. Climbing those steps showed me that I was determined to fight my fears. Having siblings taught me about relationships. Seeing my father hustle sideline jobs taught me that no matter what job you hold, it's still a job and you should be proud of it. Your job description should not define who you are! You shouldn't be embarrassed! Celebrating your birthdays and womanhood. Celebrate you, celebrate the small achievements, celebrate life!

4

THE WEDDING

I had tons of dreams to be fulfilled, dreams I wished to see.

To my dismay those dreams had to come to a sudden halt. This is where my story begins; there is no end to this story because every day from here on out was an experience and a learning curve.

Everything ended just there, no more dreams, no more nothing. "I built dreams for the future but never looked at the present".

We had to attend a wedding in November 1999, it was my mum's younger sister's wedding. I noticed that mum and dad started having frequent arguments. My parents had a major argument before mum could leave for Johannesburg and I had to tend to my brother and sister. My dad was not at all abusive, but dad did have a terrible temper. I wish I had known then what caused their sometimes little, sometimes major arguments.

Mum and Dad used to talk to me and complain about each other. Thinking I could solve whatever was going on in their personal lives, I would allow myself to tell dad what mum said and vice versa. I thought that they would realize how much they loved each other, but the arguing would stop, and then start up again.

I am not at all sure if I did make it worse, but I sure feel like I did.
I was writing my final exams in Standard 5 (Grade 7), so I could not leave with my mum and siblings for Johannesburg. I also noticed that it was the first time my dad had allowed my mum to go somewhere without him.

Remember in my previous chapter I mentioned that my dad didn't allow us to go on holidays separately? The rule was that we always went together as a family. This time, the rule was broken. It did not apply in this situation. Should I have been worried? As a 12-year old what would I know? How could I have known that this environment I was brought up in, had started to change. It changed so quickly, I never took note!

Before my mum and siblings left for Johannesburg, something strange happened.

I can't remember the date specifically, but it was towards the evening and our house phone rang. My sister answered the call and the person on the other end of the call said, "You will never see your 9th birthday." My sister got scared and handed the phone to my dad, but by this time the call had ended. My sister was crying. I mean, who does that to a child?

Was this a threat?
Was someone watching my family?
Who was this person?

We tried to trace the call, nothing at all…

Someone was playing around, or they knew what was going to happen. Weird!

The taxi arrived the next day. My Mum and siblings got in and they were on their way to Johannesburg. It was sad to see my family split. Afterall, we went everywhere together, and this was the first time it was like this. What on earth was going on?

Only my parents knew what their quarrels were about. Children were never brought into my parents' arguments. If the fight was between adults, children should not get involved. Children were not to fight their parents' fights and were not to show any disrespect towards that person. As a child, you were still to greet that person. That's how my parents brought us up. The same went for when adults were taking, you were not to "count teeth" or "lend an ear". You were to remove yourself from adult conversation.

After my mum and siblings departed for Johannesburg, I got to see a different side of my dad. Not that he never cared or showed love, he always did, but this was different. It was like a special Daddy and Daughter time. He loved my mum dearly and his children were his world. It's true that Dads and Mums are Superheroes.

Dad took over Mum's duties while she was away with my siblings in Johannesburg.

In the mornings, Dad prepared breakfast, got me up for school, made my lunch while I got ready. Mum would plait my hair for school and I wondered if dad could do that! Surprisingly he did it with perfection.

The house felt empty without my siblings and Mum. I wished that December holidays had started already. I missed them, and all that kept us in contact was calls on the landline or dad's new Alcatel cellphone.

Hahaha, this phone was a brick, it was extremely heavy, and it still had an aerial on it. You had to pull it up for reception. But hey, as man evolved, so did technology, right?

Ono night for ouppor, Dad wao toaohing mo to fry otuff. Ho wao frying samoosa's. For the life of me, I don't remember learning to cook from my parents. I never tried or attempted to make something. All I did was eat what was prepared, or I would place an order with Mum for what I wanted to eat. I don't know what the usual age is, for a young girl to learn to cook. I did household chores, but not cooking. Dad and I left maybe two weeks after mum left. Exams were done and I was so glad!

Dad always loved leaving extremely early, before sunrise. He drove very slowly. There was not a bone in his body that wanted to speed, not even if the speed limit was 120km/hour. I have no idea where I got my "need for speed". Maybe the advanced driving helped. I don't drive recklessly. Most people seem to think that if you drive fast, you are reckless. No, I speed when I need too "drive". This is safely and responsibly, especially if I am alone and feel unsafe.

Dad stuck to below the speed limit all the way to Johannesburg. We made regular stops to eat our famous tin fish sandwiches. We never pulled over to buy food or beverages. Everything was always packed from home. We stopped for toilet breaks and to do routine checks on our little red Golf. Dad always kept a little A5 book. In there, he would jot down his Km's; start and end before filling up the tank again, and the price he paid per liter.

We arrived in Lenasia in the evening, by that time my bladder was about to explode. My Mum's eldest sister met us at the garage, and I was told to jump into her car as I was going to stay at her home. I was glad, at least I could go and relieve my bladder. My cousins and siblings were so excited to see me. My dad went to my Maternal Grandmothers home. That's were all the festivities were happening. Dad carried some of his décor stuff on the roof rack. He was always helpful and very talented in music and art.

Dad taught me Calligraphy, a very fancy way of writing. I loved using his Parker pen sets, and I guess my creative and artistic flare comes from him.

I noticed my parent's arguments continued, even at the wedding house. I consoled myself by telling myself it was normal for couples to argue. I mean, we all have disagreements. My parents were just going through something. Either too much salt in the food or too little, right? I mean, I don't know what a married couple would argue about.

But what they fought about, really baffled me. I mean, they loved each other. My parents held hands in the shopping mall, dad bought mum jewelry and gifts that made her smile, they said "I love you "all the time, they called each other "Love". How cute is that?
What could possibly be wrong?
All the quarreling did not stop us from having fun!

All our families were invited, and the night before the wedding, we all danced till the early hours of the morning. My Mum's youngest sister's wedding day had arrived. As a bride, she dressed up in her traditional outfit, which is a sari. She looked like a doll. The wedding took place at a nearby temple. My soon-to-be uncle was dressed to impress as well.

Sacred vows and traditional rituals were performed. Gifts exchanged from both sides of our families.

They were now husband and wife and the celebrations continued. My dad made all the souvenirs and wedding trays for their wedding. My dad, like I said, was very talented.

My youngest aunt was now a married lady and soon my new uncle carted my aunt off to their new home in Kinross.

We were all invited for the reception in Kinross the next day. On the day of the reception, it was just formalities, a lot of speeches and gifts exchanged, and amazing food. My sister and I loved to dance, and dance is what we did at the reception. Mind you, my sister blew everyone away with her dancing. She totally nailed it. I was so proud of her. Coming from such a strict home, I am glad that our parents allowed us a little leeway at the function. That was fun.

Time passed and our holiday was coming to an end. Before we knew it, it was time to go back home to Durban. I noticed that my parents still had their quarrels and my maternal grandmother and my mums two sisters intervened. As I've mentioned, we were brought up not to sit and count teeth while the adults spoke. So, we mostly played outside with my other cousins and just had fun.

The day we left, it seemed like everything was sorted out. My parents looked happy. Whatever it was, was sorted and we were a family again.

We drove back to Durban, but a few weeks after our arrival, I don't know what came up, but mum took all 3 of us (brother, sister and I) in a taxi to Johannesburg to my maternal grandmother's home.

I did not want to leave my father alone at home, and I cried. He told me if I didn't go with my mum, he would kill himself. He pulled out his gun and held it to his head! Dad always had a gun; it wasn't something he had recently bought. He always had it locked away in the safe with a box of bullets. We were never allowed to open the safe. The keys were always hidden.

I loved my Daddy so much, I did not want that, so I had to go. That very same night, before we left, I had given Dad a ring. It was a signet ring that I had won in a competition. I always wore it on my baby finger. That night, I removed it and handed it to my Daddy. "Daddy," I told him, "never take this ring off; whenever you look at the ring think of me. I love you, Daddy."

I handed my ring over and went to pack my clothes. We left the next day. It was not a nice ride. We sat at the back of the Taxi as it was four of us. It was so bumpy and cold. I had never taken a taxi before! That was my first experience. At the halfway house, we changed taxi's for another long drive to Johannesburg. I missed my dad, again.

Something felt hollow, like the time my mum and siblings left for Johannesburg.

Why was this happening?
Why was my family breaking?
Why were my parents not happy?
What changed in 1999?

The class of 1999 Matriculant boys. That's what changed!
Those who knew, kept quiet. Even family. Assumption or not, thus far, whatever I have heard, I'll hold those who knew, accountable. You know who you are!

Dad called almost every day to check up on us. On one particular day, I had asked about our dog. Our dog's name was Snoopy.

Snoopy was hilarious and fun loving. He hated bath time and had issues with the blow-dryer. He was a Poodle, white and grey in color, his fur covered his eyes. We had to always cut the long hair away so he could see. Snoopy loved playing chase, he would run around the garden like a race horse, through the back door out the front door, up the stairs, down the stairs and then pause. And start all over again. He was so cute and funny at the same time.
He was well behaved and never went out the gate unless called.

Dad was not very fond of Snoopy, but the rest of us loved him.
I asked my dad, "How is Snoopy"? He responded with, "Snoopy ran out the gate and I was unable to find him." My heart sank and I wondered if Snoopy was ok.

It came as a shock to me because Snoopy never went out the gate, as I've mentioned.

I sat up late at night, sometimes thinking with my 12-year-old brain.

What was going through my dad's head?

Why did he lose his temper when they had small arguments?

Why did he send us away?

Why were the adults around me not telling me anything?

Everything was kept a secret. It's still like that. I understand the adult-child thing which applied back then, but I am no longer a child. At some point they could have told me or explained to me what was going on. I really needed answers.

It just puzzled me so much that, during all my years of knowing my dad, I had never seen anything like this. I mean, he always had a gun. It was always locked away in a safe and the keys hidden. But recalling the way he pulled it out and held it to his head. I hoped that everything was going to be okay with my parents and whatever it was would be resolved. I felt helpless that I couldn't make anything better between them. After all, they were my parents and I wanted them to resolve their issues so we could be a family again. We could be happy together.

Dad came up the following week. I heard through the grapevine that my Dad spoke to my mums' sisters about killing all of us in the car and setting it alight with all of us dead inside it. He bought so many bullets, the boot of the car was full. Apparently, he showed my eldest aunt. He planned to kill all that was close to him from my mum's family, including himself. I am still not sure if this was even true. You know, sometimes grapevines break or become rotten.

They spoke to him and sorted stuff out, Mum and Dad sorted out their differences while they were there at my maternal grandmother's house.

Soon things were back to normal. My parents were all happy and ready to leave for Durban. I was really excited. Finally, I would get to go home to the family that I was used to. Little did I know, that was not my fate.

I was told to stay back at my mums' eldest sisters house because I needed to be straightened up due to having a big mouth. This disheartened me a great deal because I missed my home, I missed my family time and now this. Seriously, my siblings wanted to stay with me, but dad said "no". Once dad spoke, it was final. There was no speaking back or trying to argue. No was no! What confused me, was that if I did have a big mouth, I'm pretty sure my father would have straightened me out. What on earth was going on?

He put them in the car. It looked like a scene from a movie. How a parent will just take his children shove them in the car while they are crying their hearts out to stay back with their sister, kicking, and screaming their guts out. My heart broke seeing my siblings cry to be with me. Even though we begged dad to leave my siblings behind, he refused to do so.

It was my first time staying away from my family. To make things worse, we were a whole +- 600km away from each other. I missed my brother and sister dearly. Maybe this would teach me not to fight with them. Maybe this was my lesson to be learnt. Although I had my three cousins two girls and a boy, I missed my home. I wanted my hugs, the goodnight kisses and the "I love you" tuck-in. My aim was to enjoy my holiday and maybe I could get to go home sooner than planned.

My parents had called me now and then to see how I was doing. I asked them when they would come to pick me up because I missed home and my family a lot. "Soon." was all I heard.

I had fun with my cousins. Either way I had to make it worthwhile.
My parents called me one night to congratulate me on passing Standard 5 (Grade 7). Which meant I was going to high school. What great news! I was overjoyed on hearing this news. I had obtained A's in all my subjects, except the C I got for English. But that was still good enough.

Mum said she was proud of me and would buy me the charm bracelet I had always wanted.

The charm bracelet story comes from the days of going to the ABH Chatsworth fair. We always looked forward to attending the fair. It was such an extravagant affair. To set the scene, the grounds close to the Chatsworth stadium was filled with food stalls, a stage for live music and dances, stalls that sold jewelry, makeup, junk food, games that you would win prizes and a theme park with all these rides. It was amazing. The atmosphere was just brilliant.

Dad would give us all money to spend on whatever we wanted, be it toys, play games or save it, it was entirely up to you. I loved jewelry. I always admired my mum's jewels and hoped I, too, could have my own. I had my eyes set on this beautiful charm bracelet. It was just perfect in every way. The charms were light and dainty looking. I loved it, it was perfect. As you know, you shouldn't just shop at one stall. You walk around and check prices, but I didn't care about the other stalls, I wanted that one. It was imitation jewelry and almost every stall had a replica but not that one with those charms. The night ended and I didn't get it. Hence mum's promise that she would get me one. Finally, I would get that charm bracelet! I had waited a long time for this, so you should know the excitement in the little me. It was a "happy dance" moment.

My parents always encouraged us to do well at school, and praised us when we did, so when we did extremely well in our School reports, we would get a gift. If you want something, work hard and you shall receive it. It was bribery in a way, but in the end we all got what we needed. Tricky business, I tell you.

That very same night when Mum called, I had asked her what Dad was doing. I found it strange that he hadn't called me after receiving my results. She told me he was busy cleaning his gun.

Mummy had also mentioned that they had bought Christmas presents for my brother and sister. My sister got a beautiful doll with a cradle and a bottle. Mum mentioned that my brother received a car and it was parked on the road. I believed mum, but it was not as big as mummy had described it. It was one of those small ones that you can sit on and push yourself with your legs, it had a face on it and its color was red and yellow. It also had a steering wheel with a hooter. Mum said my brother called it "BRUM". There was a program on TV which had cars that talked, and the main car's name was BRUM. We loved watching it. It fascinated us that cars could talk. My brother probably thought that this "Brum" will talk too!

Now, with all these festivities going on at home, you can imagine my cry to be at home with my parents and siblings. I was eager to go home. Mum also told me that Tasha and Shivenn were playing outside and they were smashing snails it so happened that Tasha was finding the snails and Shivenn was smashing them and Tasha mistakenly put her finger there and Shivenn, thinking it was a snail had smashed her finger with the stone. They were having fun and I wanted to go home. My sister's finger was blue from the smash.

I needed to go home, no matter what. So much excitement and drama. That longing grew to go home, to be with my family. To be with my mum, my dad, my brother and my sister. It's not something that can and will ever be replaced. My siblings spoke to me for a bit and then we said our goodbye's. Dad didn't speak to me but assured me he would call soon.

What I didn't know was that this was actually the last time I would hear their voices.

How crazy is that? Imagine speaking to someone today and the next day, or week, they are no longer! That week went by. My eldest aunt that I was staying with had planned to go camping for the weekend of 11 December 1999. As I have never been on such a holiday, I looked forward to going on this adventure. It would be something new to experience and I loved nature. Sleeping in a tent, telling scary stories, roasting marshmallows, no electricity or TV and sitting by a fire and just chilling outdoors. I just could not wait for that day. I loved that I had company to take my mind off things, even though it still bothered me.

Why did I have to stay behind?
What was the real reason?

During the weeks staying in Johannesburg with my eldest aunty and her family, not once was I disciplined or called in to be given a talk. So why did I really remain behind in Johannesburg?

Was it because my Dad saw that their arguments troubled me and made an excuse?
Was this part of his master plan?

These questions drowned my brain. When I got home, I would defiantly ask my Dad. I wanted answers for his move.
Whenever we played Chess together, he always asked me "Why did you move that?" and I had to explain. So, like with chess, I needed an explanation in order to understand. The opportunity to get answers never came.

REFLECTION

Not every marriage is a happy marriage, apply caution as too who you let in. Involving family sometimes isn't the greatest idea in resolving issues, rather seek professional assistance. A neutral person to intervene is the best as no sides are taken. Setting goals are important as it helps to keep track of where you are going and what you want to achieve. It's ok to have a little fun, put that favorite song on and dance like nobody is watching.

5

TRAGEDY STRIKES

Please note that this chapter contains details of the murder-suicide that took my family. It may be traumatic to read.

On 11 December 1999, we had all woken up early to pack. My cousins and I were really excited. I was going camping! How awesome was this holiday? The day seemed so perfect: sunny, cloudless day, birds chirping and passing stories as you walk past them, trees swaying as the cool breeze brushed through their leaves, and a sight that I could not miss, was a mother bird feeding her babies.

Our bags were lined up and ready to go. My cousins and I were all dressed up and ready to hit the road. The car was packed, house cleaned, and we were just waiting for some friends to arrive.

It was now 10:00. As we were rounding up the stuff, we got a phone call from my dad. I did not get a chance to speak to him, but after the phone call, I noticed my eldest aunt feeling a bit uneasy. It did occur to me that something was wrong but I could not gather what.

My eldest aunt announced that we were not going camping after all. Another phone call from dad. This time, I heard some words being exchanged from my eldest aunt's side of the conversation which seemed very tense. It baffled me, because she wouldn't tell me what was going on and she wouldn't allow me to speak to my dad. I mean, if there was something going on, surely if I was given the chance, I would be able to change his mind. But no, I was told to stay away. All I heard from where I was standing was the following: "Des! Go for a drive, cool down", "don't do that, they're innocent."

The conversation went on. Apparently, the last words to my eldest aunt from my dad was that she should say her last words to my mum, because they would never see each other again. My eldest aunt had mentioned she could hear my brother and sister screaming for help in background, saying "Mosi save us" (Mosi means mother's sister). At 14:50, we heard from my dad for the last time. My eldest aunt in a panic finally told me what was going on.

"Your father is holding your mother and the children hostage in the house. He tied them up with the curtain to the bed so they can't move. All the doors are locked and he is going to kill them."
I was stunned on hearing all of this.

"My dad can't do that!" I said.

This cannot be my dad. My dad was my hero, the first God of my life. He couldn't just decide to do this. I mean was he not thinking of me at this moment? This was just a joke. They were probably on their way to Johannesburg to fetch me. I kept telling myself that this was a joke. That was not my dad. That was not the dad I knew.
Time passed. We tried to contact the police in Durban, to break down the doors so at least they could save one or all of them. They refused

to co-operate. Even in the situation that we were in. People all the way from Johannesburg were trying to save people in Durban. We had explained to the police that there were two innocent children that were going to die. We begged and pleaded over the phone to please help us. The police service was so pathetic, I couldn't even believe it. All they could say was that they needed permission to break in. We gave them the permission, but they needed a person to be there. All of us were disgusted with what we heard. People's lives were at stake and they couldn't do anything. We then called my mum's brother. My mum and dad hadn't kept in contact with my Mama (Mama is mother's brother) from the time my sister was born. My dad and my Mama had a mechanical business going. I don't know what happened, but we stopped visiting them. My dad told me once that my Mama still owed him money from when they started up the business, and he hadn't kept his word. I didn't find anything new there. My Mama did not even know where we stayed. Directions were passed over the phone.

My aunt told me to sit by the phone and wait for any news.

From 15:00, I sat there waiting for some news. I started to bite my nails, a terrible habit that my dad hated. The phone rang and I answered it. It was my Mama. He did not tell me what was the situation there, and only wanted to talk to his sister. When my eldest aunt got back, I gave her the message and she dialled her brother's number. I left the room.

She received some news at around 17:00, which was confirmed by the police. It took the people we leave our lives to when in danger, two hours to get to my house. Where I had stayed in Chatsworth to where the police station is, is only a 10 minute drive.

Through all that time of this news being shared in the house, I tried to keep it together.

I sat outside for a while and thought that if whatever was said in the house earlier was true, then I need to be strong for everyone. I watched the clouds float by. I remember the breeze on my face, the birds happily chirping and the sun on my brown skin. I prayed. I hoped the Divine out there heard it and would give me the strength I needed. Eventually, I decided that sitting outside wasn't going to solve anything or give me an answer, so I decided to go back into the house. As I stepped into the kitchen, I heard people sobbing. I walked into my eldest aunt's room and she cried frantically.

It was at that moment that I realized I had lost my entire family.

I lost the four most loving and important people in my life.

My body went cold when I heard the news. My world crumbled, my heart shattered. This feeling inside of me made me sick. The pain I felt from my heart and the huge bubble in my throat. I dropped to my knees and cried. All those emotions and shock to my system. My head was spinning. Everyone around me was crying hysterically.

I cried my way to the lounge, accompanied by my eldest aunt's friends. I wanted my mummy and I wanted my mummy now! Nobody could console me. My tears just ran out of my eyes. Soon my nose was blocked. I felt the air around me get thick and I found it hard to breathe.

I remember going on like a song on repeat.

I kept on saying: "I want my family." "I want my mummy here right now." Before I knew it, I was gasping for air. The people around me, trying to calm me down saying, "Alicia, it's ok, stop crying." I tried, but I did not have any control.

A lady drove me to the nearest doctor to get something to calm me down. I did not know what was going on. I just wanted my mummy.

When I got back to my eldest aunt's house, neighbors were there to help console us and lend a hand. The scene in my head was so vivid, yet like a blur. I just saw bags being taken out, clothes being packed and arrangements were being made to leave for Durban.

Families and friends were called, to spread the news of the Late Sewdass Family of Chatsworth.

Radio stations were to announce the message on air for those we could not reach. I was told to relax and see if I could sleep, but my mind wouldn't allow me to do that!

Why was I crying?

I mean there was a possibility of my family still being alive! The insanity was surreal. I had to keep myself sane.

My thoughts told me it was a lie. They are still alive. It's only a lie. They are waiting for you to come home. You know your father wouldn't do such a thing and leave you behind. I made up things in my brain. Everyone around me dealt with this news differently and I couldn't be bothered about anyone but myself and getting home.

We left my eldest aunt's residence to find my second aunt. We could not get hold of her and we all wanted to leave together. We made a stop at my Ma's house (Maternal Granny). Ma was sick and asleep with her phone off the hook and no one could get hold of her. The news of my late family sent Ma into a state of shock. My Ma and Nana (Maternal Grandfather) packed and locked up. We had to find my second aunt. This aunt had taken care of me after my Mum gave birth to me. We eventually got hold of her and we left for the journey we will all never forget.

My cousins unfortunately didn't come along. They stayed over with their paternal grandparents. They were young and all of this wasn't something they should be exposed to, let alone try to make sense of the situation and the loss of their Aunt, Uncle and cousins who they were so fond off.

The questions continued to flood my head.
How much courage did it take to do all of this?
What was dad going through for him to do this?
Did my dad think of me?
How do you bring yourself to this point?
Why?
Did Dad reach out for help?
Why? I mean were we not a happy family?

It just kept playing on my mind over and over that this was all a joke. I prayed that it was all just a lie. I was scared.

If this was true, who would look after me?
Would they love me, or hurt me?
Where would I stay?

I was so scared. I just wanted to be in my mum's arms. I needed to be comforted by my mum.

Soon the traveling was over and it was time to face my nightmare. My stomach was turning. I felt sick. I didn't know what to expect. I still remember, I laughed on the inside, telling myself that my family was pulling my leg.

We reached my house about 03:00 on Blue Jill Crescent, Chatsworth. Silence crept deep into the early parts of the morning, I could only hear sniffs and see tears rolling down known and unknown faces. I was greeted with sorrow by family members.

As a Ritual in a Hindu home, when a loved one passes away, you put a white cloth on the floor. This is where the body will lie. The next day, when the deceased body arrives home, their head must face North and their legs must face South. The reason for facing South is because that is the direction we pray for our ancestors that have passed on. The place is known as Pitru Loka (realm between heaven and earth, a place where Pitrus go after death), and a Diya must be lit (Diya is a clay lamp filled with ghee and a cotton wool wick) and that clay lamp must stay alight through all the days of mourning. Agarbathi (incense sticks) are also used.

I still remember the smell of the incense sticks used on that day. The scent has never left my nose, I can't stand the smell. These days if I do get a whiff of it, it takes me right back to that day.

The house was dead, no pun intended. People just stood around crying. I thought we were all mad, standing and crying to our hearts content because I still believed my dad could not be capable of doing all of what they say he did. I held back my tears because it could not at all be true. At some point, I just couldn't cry. My eyes felt like sandpaper.

I was escorted into my home by my Mama. He took me upstairs to the bedroom, where the whole incident took place. They needed some legal documents and he hoped I knew where they were kept. Mind you, I did not know about policies, ID books, marriage certificates etc. It was gibberish to me. I was only 12 and I didn't know about all these things that adults kept. My Parents never told or taught me that in case of an emergency, if any documents are needed this is where you look. I only knew that if dad was driving and if a stone hit the window, or there was an attempted hijacking, he told us to stay low in the back seat. That was the only safety I knew. "Hide in case of danger."

My parents and siblings' bodies had already been taken to the morgue. I was hoping that I could see my family! It hit me hard as a rock. I WAS ALONE IN THIS WORLD.

It felt so weird to go home and nobody was there to greet me the way it always happened. The smell of my mummy's perfume in her room comforted me a bit. I scratched around, looking for what was requested, but I didn't find what was really needed.

My Mama had explained to me in what positions my family were found in, as he was the first person there with the police. Looking back, I'm not sure it was a good idea to explain that to a 12-year-old. My mind needed answers and I started drawing pictures of what had been!

The following is especially sensitive as this is the scene of how my family was found according to the first response.

In the main bedroom, my mum and baby brother were found. Mum was on the bed with a pillow over her head, my little brother on the floor with his hands covering his head.

In my bedroom that I shared with my sister, were my dad and baby sister.

It looked like my sister tried to jump through the window, according to the scuff marks left on the wall. I don't know. She probably tried to act busy by reading a book, because a book lay open on my bed, my dad was found on my sisters' bed.

According to what was explained to me, I tried to picture this all. As I have mentioned, I drew a picture of the scene in my mind. They all had, had a gunshot wound on their heads.

I felt sick to the absolute core of my soul. The air started becoming thick and I felt my chest and nose shut down.

WHAT THE HELL WAS MY FATHER THINKING?
WHAT THE HELL HAS JUST HAPPENED IN MY HOME?

There were blood stains everywhere. In my room alone, the ceiling, computer, floor, bed, curtains, walls, the entire Childcraft Encyclopedia collection, and our cupboards. The bathroom had blood. In the main bedroom, my mum's blood soaked into the mattress and my brother's blood covered the floor.

I wished so hard that someone could slap me really hard to bring me back to reality. This messed up disaster of a scene had to be a joke. It was a joke! I wanted out of this dream NOW! I felt so sick. To make myself believe this wasn't at all real, I told myself it was tomato sauce smeared everywhere, and that my family was hiding somewhere, ready to pounce on me when I turned away.

I could not come to terms with believing that my family was no longer! That I WAS ALONE!

I stood in my room, looking at everything, thinking of how this had played out. I needed proof, I thought to myself.

I NEEDED PROOF!
What other way to get proof? I needed to have a look under those curtains to see if what was said was true to the eyes. Eyes cannot deceive! I built up the courage and picked up one of the curtains from my sister's bed. It was drenched with blood. I could not handle what I had seen and the smells that lurked in the house, the air felt thick again and I couldn't breathe, the dead night made me sick. I fainted

in my room. My Mama carried me out of my home for some fresh air and space.

I felt empty, the warmth from my soul was kicked out into the dead night. So much was going on around me. All I wanted was my bed, my parents and siblings. Their hugs and warmth. That was all I wanted.

In those few hours that I sat outside, I still couldn't comprehend that all this had happened.

I still did not believe what I saw. If someone is dead, we need to see or view their body, right? Well, then that's what I would wait for. My next step was to see their bodies. I am sure then I would believe this whole saga.

I was in Denial. I was in one of the first steps of grief. I didn't know it then.

I still could not believe that my dad actually shot them. Now I spoke out of anger in my head. He shot my mum first, then my brother and sister and lastly himself and all were shot in the head.

Why daddy?
Why?
Why?
Why?
He left me alone in this world.
No mother;
No father;

No brother;
And no sister.
He left me all alone.

I stayed over at my Mama's place. I did not sleep, it was no use. When I got up the next morning, he gave me all the valuables that were found on their bodies. I took my dad's spectacles, which still had blood on them. I remember this because somebody took them away from me at some point in the upcoming days, saying there was blood on the spectacles. My mum's jewelry lay there but one piece had caught my eye! It was the ring I gave my daddy to wear. Remember the ring I gave to my Daddy, I told him to never take it off? He died with the ring on his finger.

I HOWLED. You know that hollow, painful cry that hurts so bad? My Mama's wife at that time helped me to bath. I was numb. Food wasn't even a priority. I cried until I couldn't anymore. That heartache just didn't leave.

Why daddy? Why did you do this?
I held onto those spectacles for dear life. It felt like I was holding my dad close to me, even though they were spectacles. They were non-existent to me the day before.

On 12 December 1999, the day of the funeral, I anxiously waited, eager to see their bodies. This would be the confirmation I needed. It was either that they were dead, or alive. Or just putting on a show. I felt we had no privacy. Journalists from everywhere were there, watching the house, and us, like birds of prey.

I mean this family, my family, were busy mourning the death of 4 dear ones and they just needed to capture their story. Was it all worth it for their weekend headlines around South Africa? I understand that this was their job, but they could at least have shown some respect. They kept asking this question and that question, for goodness sake.

When the bodies arrived, we had all walked up to the garage. And I saw. I saw their lifeless bodies, just lying there, in their coffins.

I wanted to run away.

THIS ISN'T MY FAMILY. NOPE, NOT MINE.

Can this be my worst nightmare that has now turned into reality? Are these 4 coffins a dream, or is it true that this tragedy has actually taken place? At first, I refused to go close to the coffins. I was scared. Is that my family? I was shattered. I could not handle what I saw. The tears no longer had space in my eyes, they moved out, one-by-one. A river ran down my cheeks. It took me some time to build up the courage to get close to their lifeless bodies.

"Dad wake up. It's me, ALICIA!"
"Daddy, please wake up. It's me."
I shouted till my voice was silent.
"Mummy, wake up. I need a hug!"
"Mummy!" I shouted.
I had lost them all. I was broken beyond repair.

I tried to get them up they wouldn't move. Their bodies were so cold.

No warmth left. Mummy and my sister's coffins were placed on top of each other, and Dad and my brother's placed the same.

My mum lay there, beautiful as ever, adorned in a beautiful sari. My sister was dressed in a Punjabi. Her chest was so big. It looked as if they had stuffed her body with sponge, for it to blow up the way it did. My brother looked so cute in his coffin, like a real angel, ready to be received at the gates of heaven. Both the kids where so innocent in their coffins. How could dad do this to them?

Imagine how they must have felt when dad had fired the first shot that killed my Mummy! What did my siblings do when they saw what my dad had threatened, was true, that he was going to kill them?

The panic that must have set in their little souls.

After dad killed mum, who was going to be next?
Did my siblings fight back?
Did my siblings suffer?
Did their screams and cries matter to dad?
How did the kids run away from him?
He was coming to kill one of them, but who?
My brother was next. A small, innocent 3-year-old that had not even seen life. He was still a baby. My brother, Shivenn. My baby brother was gone.
Did my baby brother feel pain when he was shot?
Did he struggle and die?
To date, I keep thinking of the image I had painted in my head, as described by my Mama on that day.

Shivenn had his hands over his head in a fetus position. He was a baby, a baby Dear God. My Soul. How my heart aches writing this. The pain I am feeling doesn't do any of this any justice. He was just a baby. Only 3-years-old and in a week's time he would have celebrated his 4th birthday.

My sister, Tasha, was next.
Did my sister run?
Was she still tied?
Did she have an asthma attack?
The scene showed a book open on the bed. Scuff marks on our wall. My talented, beautiful sister. What did you go through after witnessing 2 deaths?

Then my dad. The last to take his life. I don't know what it is that made him do this.

Why daddy?
Why take everyone and leave me?
Just imagine a father that has to pull a trigger on his wife and 2 kids.
The guts needed to pull the trigger.
Held at gun point!
What did a 3 and 8-year-old do?

Well surely, it's a scary feeling for us all. A gun held to your head(temple). What thoughts run through your head in those few seconds, waiting for the trigger to be pulled? The feeling is dark. You just wait and think silently, pull the trigger already. Hearing the sweat dripping from your dad, as it drips and hits the floor with a splash.

74

What a scary feeling.

They did not even say goodbye to me!
I felt lonely, hurt, let down and abandoned.
Questions poured out from I don't know where.
Why did this have to happen to me?
How will I cope?
I think I have died a million times every second since their death.

I stood there at one stage, blank minded, just looking at my family. My Aunties, crying for their sister that they loved so much, my Ma and Arji (Maternal and Paternal grandmother) shattered.

It's hard to believe that one's child can pass away before you.
A child you had carried for 9 months, you've seen him/her crawl, walk, run, their first words, school, marriage, grandchildren and now their daughter and a son are gone forever. I felt so sorry for them both.

My Arji stayed with my dad's younger brother in Port Shepstone. The only people I knew from my daddy's family was my Arji and Aaja, Dad's younger and eldest brother, my dad's sister and a few of Dad's cousins. I knew how everyone felt that day. I felt their pain but I was helpless.

This was now my reality.

All their bodies were taken to the school where my dad had taught.

I remember walking in last, accompanied by someone. As I entered the school courtyard, the entire school stood in honor of my daddy. So many students and teachers came to say goodbye to my father, Mr H Sewdass.

Oh, Daddy you were loved so much. Why did you do this? Why did you take away the lives of three and your own?

I was given a seat at my dad's head side.
As people walked by, I sat there crying and I still attempted to wake my dad. I kissed him on his forehead so many times. I was greeted with the cold from his lifeless body. I held onto his spectacles. The funeral procession left for the crematorium. We followed along with our close family.

As their bodies were transported to the crematorium, I just sat and cried.

I knew my life was going to change after this.
Their bodies were laid on the conveyer, I had to say my goodbyes.

THIS WAS MY FINAL GOODBYE!

How does a 12-year-old bid her family farewell?
How could I allow them to be cremated?
What were the chances of them still being alive?
I panicked and threw a tantrum. I could not witness this. My heart ached. It was a final goodbye.
A final goodbye, don't take them away from me.

I wanted my mummy. "Just bring her back to me! Bring my family back." was all I uttered.

It was just me with my numb body and my emotionless soul.

The bodies of my loved ones were cremated. Traditional ceremonies followed over the next few days. I don't remember what happened after the crematorium. All I know is that I was sad.

We stayed over at my youngest aunts, mother-in-law's home. I remember that I couldn't eat. Just a few bites of a butter bread sandwich and some tea was all I kept in. I felt sick to the core.

The next day, some of the remaining rituals were performed. I sat with a blank face. All I felt was my tears rolling down my cheeks.

After the third day ceremony was over, it was time to pack up. We had to pack all my late family's belongings. Clothes were donated to the orphanage, furniture given away or sold, the same with ornaments and tools. We kept only certain things of sentimental value, or things we had place for to cart to Johannesburg.

People helped themselves to my parents' things. I just watched in disgust. We had the most beautiful garden. Don't be too surprised, but people were literally pulling plants out of the garden. I know you want some sort of "something" to remind you of my late family but that is not the way to do it, it's not!

Not for me or anybody.

I was moving to Johannesburg. I understood that not everything could be taken. There was no time to even say goodbye to my friends.

Certain things were left behind in Durban because it was too much to take back with us. We left behind the lounge suite, dining room table with its matching chairs and divider, both our fridges and a freezer. My Ma's sister was kind enough to let us leave it all at her home. And, as time went on, we could decide what to do with it.

About a day or two after we had sorted everything out, we left for Johannesburg. It was sad to lock up the house that I had once lived in. To turn my back and walk away. That was once my home. My siblings and I played there, my mum prepared beautiful meals. All that was just gone. I held onto my memories.

The house we once lived in, was now only lived in by darkness and sadness. The walls spoke to themselves and not to three small children who once wrote on them with their laughter.

Walls which now only hold memories and that have witnessed what happened, stay quiet, afraid to speak. The people who once looked after the house are now only the shadows that dwell in dark and not the happiness and sunlight that once shone through every window. And don't forget the child that had to start all over. A child that had to face the world without her family. How do I do this? I am just 12 years old!

"Death took over the house, memories alive in mind, but life must go on!"

Black bin bags covered the windows, doors locked. I walked away and said goodbye to an empty home.

The late Sewdass family: 11 December 1999

REFLECTION

Death.. the end to the cycle of life and a new cycle to the afterlife. Allow yourself to mourn, it is ok to let those emotions out. There will be anger, denial and endless questions. Guilt tripping, blaming yourself, something you could have done to save them or you may have been blamed for the death of your loved one! Remember it was something that this person chose, it is not your fault. I have often heard "just deal with it", "you will get over it!" It just makes it worse for the person mourning. Learn how to deal with a Suicidal person. Don't say things like, "don't go do something stupid", "you are a coward", "you are weak", "you are inconsiderate to take your life". This might be the last straw that the person is holding onto.

Those words can cause the person to go ahead with their suicide. Rather ask if they would like to talk about what they are going through. Can you offer any assistance? Even if you just listen without passing judgement. Just let them know that they are needed.

6

DAYS TO COME

Darkness filled the air, my body, mind and soul. Was there a need to smile, laugh, sing and dance again? Days went by. I sat in my own blank mind, wondering what went wrong. How could this be possible? Why now?

Nobody could answer my questions!
People knew the answers to every question I had, but due to the fact that they knew what went on that day, they keep it to themselves.

I had a hard time coming to terms with what had happened. But no one understood what was going on, on the inside of me. What they saw was their observation and that's it. I felt that many people had forgotten what had happened and soon moved on quite quickly.

Everyone deals with grief in their own way, I guess. Being so emotionally affected, the slightest things triggered me to cry. Especially when I was shouted at.

At night, I would cry myself to sleep. My heart felt like it was ripped open and left to cry out all the blood it pumped to keep me alive. My pillow became my best friend, absorbing all those silent words and tears. I lived in a body that made me walk, talk, smile and sleep but the inner me died. I failed to live within me, I failed to keep them alive I let myself down. I felt I had let my siblings down as well. I couldn't save them.

I was taken for counseling. It was done by a social worker. I think I attended two sessions and it was stopped. It was just me in my world now. The lonely me. I dreamt of them every night, and I would wake up in a shock on hearing the gun shots that were fired on that day, or I would see myself walking up the stairs of my house to the bedrooms and seeing my family lying in their frozen positions. I lived to see another day but would I live further?

NO!!!

I needed my family I needed to be with them. This voice inside of me just kept on telling me go ahead and commit suicide. DO IT! I actually thought of ways in my head to kill myself.

I did not build up the courage to do so.

I stayed with my eldest aunt for about 1 ½ years. During this time, I learnt that I was an orphan, a person that has no parents, and that family can really end up being nasty. At least that is in my view, others would beg to differ. They would say that I was treated well and I should be grateful and should understand it must have been hard for my aunt to take care of me. My maternal family took full responsibility for taking care of me, and since I was left in the care of my eldest aunt, she had felt it was her right to take on the role.

My family gave me all the support I needed BUT they could and would not replace my family.

"The amount of love given by family and friends is just enough to keep you going for each day, but it will never match that of your original family (mum, dad, sister, brother)"

I stayed with my three cousins and my eldest aunt and her husband. They lived in Johannesburg. Their street was always lively. There were often children on the streets, riding their bikes, playing games, guys driving their cars with loud music that would make your house windows vibrate. The street of life. They had really nice neighbors, who always knew everyone's business. They knew all the stories of each and every house on that street. The neighbors were our own journalists that kept us posted on who was dating who, who was pregnant, why one uncle divorced his wife. The bond formed with these neighbors were priceless, they were very caring and supportive when it came to advice, helping to attend to the kids, cook food for us when we came home from school and a lot more. Instead of having one mum we had a few!

We had a tuck shop next door to us. That was really nice and so was the aunty there. The opposite neighbor made speaker boxes and built-in cupboards. These people had the most beautiful garden on the street and another house diagonally opposite our house was an aunty who taught Bharanarthium (a traditional Indian dance).

Our Kitchen neighbors were our talk-over-the-wall pals. I loved every moment of standing on the buckets just to chit-chat. I never did that in my home in Durban. Dad did not entertain such talk and it was not considered good behavior.

My brother's birthday was on 18 December 1999. He would have been 4 years old.

Christmas came sooner than expected, or at least it had felt that way. Christmas was sad, dull and gloomy we spent time at my aunt's friend's house. We had a braai and there was a lot of alcohol. It was time to eat and a song played that my mum loved as I ate, I swallowed a tear, tears rolled down my cheeks. One of the children spotted me trying to eat and hiding my tears away. Aunty was summoned and she came to see what was wrong. All I heard was;

"Hey, Alicia knows where and when to perform." I was fragile and emotional. Being in public meant suppressing my emotions.

I thought I would be comforted by a hug and kiss but those words added its first scar to my new heart! Maybe you did not understand what you did, but thank you, that day you made me open my eyes to so much more of your hurt.

Before that day, I never knew how intense it was. But though they couldn't see the world through my eyes, I will allow them to see it now.

"We all have eyes, different colors, and shapes. They look alike now and then and we say there isn't any difference we all can see. It's a lie, because what I see, you can never see and vice versa. Put yourself in my position, walk in my shoes, feel what I feel and see what my eyes see. Then, only, will you know."

For New year's, my cousins and I spent time with some other cousins. We were ready to welcome the year 2000. We prepared a terrible mixture which contained: eggs, sauce, coloring, flour, and a lot of other rotten stuff. Mmmmm!!! It smelt terrible. Can you smell it???

I would have felt sorry for myself if I had to get messed with that stuff, and the smell would most probably take forever to get off. It was my first New Year's Eve without my family and I wanted to cry my heart out. I had mastered putting on a mask so I wouldn't get shouted at for "a performance."

Midnight arrived and the doors locked. No one was outside and I thought I would be the first to mess everyone. Boy, was I in for a surprise! My cousins were hiding upstairs on the balcony. I could not see them and a bucket-full of goo was in there, ready to fall on me, and it did!

We all had so much fun! Shoe polish, tomato's, everything that we found now was to mess any one we came across. Eventually it was time to wash up.

The smell of those eggs made me sick; it lasted on my hair for a week. It was just too potent.

The celebrations were done, and it was time to get some sleep and prepare to go home, which was literally 5 minutes away.

There were times when I really did feel out of place in my aunt's home, I felt uncomfortable, especially when the kids played with their parents. They jumped and laughed, and I would stand there in their kitchen, watching through the spaces in the cupboard. I kept telling myself "They are not your parents, so you cannot spoil their fun by jumping in."

How could I fit in? How?

I'd go sit in the lounge and just watch TV. I'd laugh at their fun like it didn't bother me. My cousins were so lucky. A lot of things I did with my parents came to a sudden halt living in another home. I know that not everyone in a family is like this. But I had a very different experience which made me hate it in the end. It troubled me a lot when I saw children with their parents, because I longed for that connection. That pain was just on a different level altogether. I wish for no child to feel this pain. My heart went out to the orphans around the globe. How did they manage?

Yes, I was with family. Yes, it was my mum's sister, but it was not my place.

Time changed, days went by, seasons changed and so did people's attitudes towards me. I never lacked anything at my Aunt's house for the first couple of months. There was a change after a while and I saw I was treated differently, but I left it to blow over. My cousins and I had loads of fun. I felt that I had to put on that smile during the day while around everyone and at night when I lay down to rest, I would cry to my heart's content.

I was grateful to my eldest aunt and her family for taking me in and it must have been a lot on her part. I know it isn't easy on anyone to just look after somebody's child. But then again, I wasn't just anybody's child, I was her niece, I was her sister's daughter. And a sister is as good as my mum, or so I thought.

I soon knew how to act and really put on a happy show, it became a norm and my new identity.

I started high school in the year 2000. I was in Grade 8. I found it really hard to adapt after the tragedy that took place and I lost concentration in school. I had new friends, and everything was just so new. It felt like I had to forget that I had just gone through such a terrible tragedy. My trauma wasn't dealt with, I didn't heal, I didn't understand so many things.

I still had so many questions that didn't have answers to and my extended family avoided speaking about my family's death to me. I was confused. I had to just jump into getting back into school and dealing with all this trauma, alone, at night. 11 December 1999 to January 2000 wasn't enough time to be ok. I was not ok. I had to grow up. I had to mature faster than I should have.

The first few days went well. I managed to make friends with someone I knew who was there as well. I was glad to have a familiar face. A childhood friend and my eldest cousin that I hadn't seen in ages attended the same school, so I felt a little less anxious. Days went by and I had to cope with everything that had happened a month before, along with, homework and school. Luckily, I made friends easily.

Grade 8 seemed like a breeze to me. I shared my story with certain friends. There were always questions about why I left Durban and moved to Johannesburg, and I was getting tired of being asked because it just brought back memories. One day, I had to do a speech in English class about my family, and in there I spoke about what I had to deal with on the 11 December 1999. My classmates then understood why I came to Johannesburg and gave me space when I needed it. As with any school, there were some meanies, and a group of boys bullied me.

What was new to me, was that I was so used to dad bringing home unused books and stationery, blank A4 papers and things like that. It actually worried me that HE wasn't around to give me these luxuries I was used to. I never knew we could purchase these things from a shop. Dad was always the supplier.

How I missed my dad and our schooling days in Durban. I was used to Dad fetching us from school and dropping us off or we would walk together to school. I now had to wait to be collected with a transport along with my cousins. I guess it's still the same thing, but no dad, no red Golf. I was so innocent minded with certain things I wondered how I could be blamed for my family's death. It puzzled me. I started learning new things and one habit that stuck was swearing. I loved swearing. I still do!

I had made enough friends to keep me happy, and I looked forward to going to school. I had fun every day. The days felt better being at school then going home. My school friends always helped me out when I didn't understand something and assisted me a lot with my assignments and projects.

I was finding my place amongst all the commotion I was dealing with in my head. The year 2000 was all about finding out where I actually fitted. What I liked and disliked. This included colors, animals, numbers, clothing and a lot more. I was a crowd-pleaser. I went with the flow and I felt that I allowed my choices to be the same as others. I never knew what I had liked. What were my favorite things? The kids around me seemed like they definitely knew themselves.

I can say that I was a copycat because I was not original. A typical example was that everyone loved blue in school. So, I loved blue too, but today I can say I actually love all colors and my favorite is yellow because it's bright like my personality. I had to learn about myself, but that came later on.

I never knew what I wanted out of my life. I just wanted to take each day as it came.
My eldest aunt had most of my parent's things, such as dad's cameras, mum's designer Indian outfits, dishes etc. I felt was nice of my aunt to keep them for me. One day, when I was older and I had my own place, I would be able to take all those things that belonged to me, to my new home. At that time that is what I had thought.

There were times, like on a hot day, we would have water fights, hose pipes and buckets of water everywhere. On some days the fun we had made me forget about my reality. I guess when the changes started happening it was because my eldest aunt could no longer take care of me. I know everyone says it must have been hard to look after an extra child and I was told many times that I was a burden to the family.

Things had changed so quickly; another level of my eldest aunts shrewdness. On returning home one day from school, I had noticed a lady walking out with one of my late mum's clothing. Some time back, I had asked if I could use my mum's clothing. My eldest aunt had said NO. But this total stranger was walking out of the yard with my mum's clothing. On closer inspection, as I walked into the house, my eldest aunt was busy distributing my mum's Indian outfits (Eastern wear) to her friends. I was so angry. I told her that those were for me, not for her to distribute at her own free will. I learnt that I definitely had no say in saving any of my mum's clothes.

Apart from clothing, I found out that my trust fund was R0.00. My parents' policies didn't pay out due to the suicide. This is what I was told, but if I look at it now, this was a murder-suicide. In my mum's situation, it was murder so I am sure something would have paid out. Later, I found out that our home was auctioned to cover my dad's debt. So, I basically came out with R0.00. Nothing was for me, or worked in my favor. All I was told at the age of 12 was that there was no money for me. So, I moved on. I decided at that point to tackle it when I was older. My Ma and my other aunts tried different lawyers and got advice and it was always a dead end. Money has never and will NEVER define the person I am today.

My home was auctioned to pay for all dad's debt and what he had owed on the house. That's what I was told. I wish I knew more at 12 years old, especially things concerning my parents' estate. Like many other thoughts, it did cross my mind that someone had obviously taken all my trust money. It could also be that there was just nothing. We will never know.

"A time will come when people will hurt and steal from someone who does not know much. Thinking that they will not at all get caught, but what they don't remember is that my parents are my guardian angels and are watching over me."

A year had gone by. I felt I was becoming a burden to my eldest aunt and her family and it was always brought up that I was a burden. Outings were cut down a lot. There were many times where I'd run my bath water and cry behind that closed door. I would try to bring myself to slit my wrists open. Some days, arguments and the things said became too much and I wished that I was dead. I wished that my life could just end. I never spoke about how they made me feel. I kept all that bottled up.

On weekends my aunt and uncle had friends over. They would consume alcohol, and dance. All the kids would be busy, always on our own mission. It was a different atmosphere because my parents didn't consume alcohol and smoke. While the night was still young, the adults would leave, normally to go to the casino. My aunt's eldest daughter and I were left to clean up and look after the younger kids. Or my Ma's brother would come to fetch me and my cousins, to spend a weekend with their children. Sometimes, we went to Water World or the casino with the adults. We gambled on the Magic Company games.

And what happened with all the left-over alcohol? We would drink it and act drunk. Maybe we were actually drunk. I experimented, and I am glad I did.

My cousin and I, being the eldest, had responsibilities and chores. We normally visited family on Sundays. I felt that my cousin (who is two years younger than me), was robbed of her family time because of me. I felt we were neglected or the reason for being left behind was because of ME.

This is what made me pay attention to being treated differently because, in the beginning, we all went together everywhere, and then it all just stopped.

I noticed that whenever they would want to go out, my eldest cousin and I would be left at home and the smaller ones would go with them.

School allowances for spending was scarce though the smaller one's always got. It was the same when it came to buying clothes. My eldest aunt told me she always treated me the same as her children, but I did not think so. Why would my eldest aunt hide and buy clothes for me and lie to her husband that it was for her? Why did people want me to stay with them if they could not handle looking after me?

My uncle's nieces always gave us their clothing that no longer fitted them. I loved those days when we got their clothes, because I knew the value of it, it didn't bother me that it was second hand. If it fitted it was mine. One day, I was even accused of stealing a R50 note. I remember leaving it clearly on the table, when my eldest aunt asked for it, it was gone and I was questioned:

"Where is the money? What did you buy with it? Why didn't you just ask if you needed money?"

What, had I now become a thief?

Later that evening, when my uncle arrived from work, he was updated on the R50 being stolen. "She probably took it to buy drugs!" So, I was supposedly on drugs too... ok!

It never ended. The false accusations never stopped.
My fight went on and I fought for myself every time. I had no one to stand up for me, but myself, and when I did answer back, it meant "I had a big mouth". I was told that, "If I wanted to act like the lady of the house, then I must go sleep in her bed and take her husband" because I wanted to have a big mouth.

I was only 12 years old, and already I realized that family can put on a huge show in front of your parents when they are alive. The day your parents are no longer, you see who your family truly is. Those masks fall away! I do hope that there are families out there that do look after their nieces and nephews like their own. I appreciated everything given to and done for me. I don't know where the dislike for me came from!

My mum and I never had arguments like this, maybe because I spoke differently to my parents. I had more respect for them and they never falsely accused me of anything, but it seemed like I wasn't the best of the crop when it came to this aunt or any of my mother's sisters. I know a child should be disciplined and I know I may have said certain things in my defense.

So maybe I did sometimes deserve to be dished out harsh words and shouted at.

There was a time I was washing dishes and we had had another argument. It got out of hand. While washing dishes I prayed that if I was wrong, I should be punished. Just a few minutes later the glass broke in my hand, cutting the skin on my baby finger open. There was a chunk of skin flapping around. I managed to put on a plaster and the skin stuck itself back. The wound had sealed. There were times, on weekends, when my cousin and I would clean the house while the others were being bathed and dressed to go shopping. I always thought if I did more, my eldest aunt would love me more. I decided to scrub the floor at the doorstep. It had white tiles and it looked brown, I had taken it upon myself to scrub it.

On my hands and knees scrubbing I succeeded in getting them white. I was so excited because I had accomplished something, I could show my aunt. Little did I know that when they arrived, it went unnoticed. Even though I showed her what I did, it was just received with a sigh. I guess I never fitted in at all. I had noticed that I was also dressed differently to her children. The longer I observed, the more I noticed all the different treatments I received.

There were good days too, not all were bad, and I wished those good days lasted. I loved them all, I just wish the adults could have shown me their love.

To be constantly reminded of "how my mother would be turning in her grave for all my wrong doings" hurt me.

Discipline me, spank me but don't say the above, that was uncalled for.

I never found a mother in my aunt, even though she is a mother but she wasn't like *my* mother. I admired her business skills and her strength, qualities I hoped one day to adopt.

I loved my cousins and I was always willing to help them with school work or chores. We loved writing on each other's backs before falling asleep. There were two single beds in the one room. So, we would sleep two on a bed. On weekends, we would join the beds to make one big bed and we would stay up to tell ghost stories. We would sleep facing a back, and we would use our index finger to draw patterns on the back in front of us. Then we would change direction so that the last person could have a turn. It was calming and we would fall asleep. Later on, the third bedroom had a bed put in. I can't remember if it was a double bed or bunk bed. We would alternate sleeping in each room. We had fun. I really missed my parents' hand cooked meals. Even though my eldest aunt had great cooking skills, it didn't come close to what I wished to taste. Somethings, I guessed, I would have to let go of.

My eldest aunt had friends that came over. Some of these friends, I had known from my childhood days. I used to confide and find peace in one Aunt that I knew well. I love her so much. The one day, I wrote this dear lady a letter. I was afraid that someone in my aunt's house would find it. So, I stuck the pages together.

Guess what? My Aunt found it. In there, I had written everything that I had felt, living with my eldest aunt and how I longed to have a motherly figure in my life. I wrote everything my heart ached and yearned for. My aunt was very angry with me due to the fact that it was a letter to one of her best friends that I felt a connection to. I was probably wrong for that as well. I apologized.

I called my eldest aunt and uncle, mum and dad. Thinking it would make it all better. I thought it would take away my pain. For some time, it felt good to actually say mum and dad. It felt real. It felt whole. I thought to myself, if I am going to live with them for the rest of my life I might as well call them mum and dad, instead of Mosi and Mosa

By this time in 2001, living with my eldest aunt was validation that sometimes you are just not wanted, but placed because of circumstances. Not everyone loves you. Maybe they do, but have a different way of showing it. You cannot ask for things or you will get shouted at. You can't ask to go out with your friends to a movie or day out. It felt like I was just a burden. It was never my place, never my home, and they were never my parents. Not even calling them mum and dad made it so.

I chose to become silent. I chose not to shine and I chose to wear black. The color black became my shadow, my hiding space, my place to be alone.

For me, being silent was the best possible option. It kept me out of trouble and I didn't have to share my thoughts with anybody, not like anyone asked. It was just me, myself and I. My light had died on the inside of me. The day my family was called to rest, I died with them. I was hurt to a point that I had become cold and emotionless.

I was angry inside.
I was angry with my dad and mum.

They left me in the so-called capable hands of my aunt.

Anger swallowed me whole. If my parents had lived to tell their story, I sure as hell would have lashed out at them for their doings.

For making me suffer and to be tortured at such a young age.

Dear Aunty,

Thank you for taking care of me. I am sure it wasn't easy to take on a fourth child into your home and it probably was costly to look after an additional mouth to feed. As many people do say "it was hard for you to take in a child like me, I should be mindful". It may seem that I wasn't grateful for all that you have done. I was. There were some days, YOUR words were so harsh in our arguments, such as when you would shout out "You killed your parents", "Your mother must be rolling in her grave".

Such words wounded me, I felt like a soldier coming home from war, holding the last bit of me together. Even though I tried, it was just not good enough.

If I look back, it was a very toxic relationship. And, dear Aunt, I know if you reading this you are probably swearing at me, and saying how ungrateful I am or was. I was not ungrateful, but grateful for the roof, food, and clothing and some of the love you and your home gave me. But in this same breath, I felt you did not honor my parents with your word. They entrusted you with taking care of their daughter. Which you failed to do. I had noticed that over time, I was treated differently than your children. I know I wasn't yours. I know you couldn't love me like my mum, I knew you hated me, because you blamed me every time for their death.

I have forgiven you for your ways but I will not forget the amount of pain you inflicted on me emotionally and mentally.
You made me feel worthless.

Nothing will change the way I feel about you.
Dislike is still a subtle word. I have forgiven you but I will not forget.
The amount of anxiety I get when I see you at a family function is validation that you have hurt me beyond repair.

REFLECTION

People need to understand that it is okay to not be okay. Grieving is a process it's not a quick fix. Change in environment can cause behavioral changes. It is okay to ask for help. It's okay to find yourself and to find your voice. Certain circumstances leave us to mature faster than others and we learn to say no! The harsh reality, not everyone is here to love you, some relationships need to be broken and we need to understand that some things cannot be replaced. We turn to "Survival mode".

7

TIME TO MOVE

My life hit a curve ball, just as I was halfway through my Grade 9 year in 2001, my eldest aunt decided that I should move to my grandparents. It confused me, because I was settled in and now, I had to move again.

Maybe I was a burden, because that was always thrown in my face.

Maybe they just couldn't afford caring for me,
Maybe other family members felt I needed better care,
Maybe I was just too much of a rebel. Whatever it was, it hurt. And I had to leave behind cousins that grew fond of me and looked up to me as an older sister.

My clothes were packed into bin bags, and I was dropped off outside the gates of my grandparents' home. Yes, I did say bin bags- there weren't any suitcases to spare. It felt like I was someone from the street, just dumped!

Remember I said I called my aunt and uncle "Mum and Dad".
After this incident, did they really deserve to be called "mum and dad"? I was not their child in the first place. So maybe to abandon

me was easier than their own brood. I had learnt so many things the hard way, and people question me today! I have heard things: "people gave you the best life." This was the best life?

Not just anybody can be called mum and dad. I thought by calling them mum and dad it would make it feel like home. But truth be told, those words are sacred to the parents given to you by our Creator. It has meaning and love when you call out to mum and dad. That's when I stopped calling them mum and dad, and I will never call anyone mum and dad, unless it is my biological parents. This caused a stir for me later on in my life. You will see why.

Standing outside with my bin bags, I cried.

Who does this? Really, who does this? My grandparents, came outside to collect me and my luggage. I was sad and heartbroken. Did my parents really leave me in this world to be treated like a piece of trash? Did my father actually think that I would be taken care of? Did my maternal family even love me like a daughter? Was this an act? Was I being punished for being a terrible daughter? Seriously, what was it? What did I do wrong to deserve this?

I was old enough to understand death, but the pain and suffering that came with being an orphan, that is another level of pain. A child sent from pillar to post, not knowing if I had to relocate again, or if anyone actually loved me. I was their late sister's daughter. I was their niece. You look up to your mum's sisters as your second mum. But sadly enough, this wasn't lived up to. Now do you understand why I fought, tooth and nail, with my maternal family? For those that had a lot to say that I always fought with my maternal family, here are all your answers to my fights that I will no longer be silenced for. That's why I say, family is so good to your face when your parents are alive. When your parents are no longer around, you are just a nothing. If you are lucky, they will treat you the way your parents did. I unfortunately was not that lucky.

This was my second heartbreak. When people or should I say family "love you" they do what is best for you. That is a load of rubbish. I was almost 14 years old when I was dropped off at my grandparents. By law, my grandparents were my legal guardians.

So, I settled down with my grandparents. It was hard at first, because my grandparents were old and from a totally different generation. My Ma still maintained a job at her age, and my Nana was an alcoholic, but a very respectful soul.

Like I mentioned, it was hard at first, to settle in again. Ma and Nana were very old school, and me being a teen, let's say that at first it was like an oil-and-water relationship. But as time went on, it got better.

I started to understand them, and they understood me. At times my Nana got too drunk, he would swear and shout at my Ma. We would just lock our room door and listen to music or watch TV.

Ma would wake up early, bath, pray, prepare my breakfast and lunch for school. Then she would wake me up to bath. It was our morning routine. In winter, she would make sure that I dressed warm. And when I mean warm, at least four long sleeve tops under my school shirt, then another two jerseys and my jacket to go over. Under my school pants I wore two other pants and two pairs of socks. And Ma would check that I was dressed warmly enough. The Johannesburg winters were extreme. I had lived in Johannesburg for almost 2 years and this *lil* Durbanite froze to the bone every winter. Don't mess with Winter! No matter how much you tried to get out of wearing so many pieces of clothing, it just didn't work. Ma would watch you dress so you didn't slip up.

If I can remember clearly, Ma started work at around 08:00 and finished around 18:00. I speak under correction. Ma walked or hitchhiked to work. In the afternoons, some customers were kind enough to drop Ma off. Thank you kind souls, for that. I would finish up my homework, so by the time Ma arrived I had enough time to help her prepare supper.

After school I would come home, clean up everywhere just so Ma didn't have extra work. I would send Nana to buy bread, chips and sweets. Whenever I had extra money, I would give Nana money to buy a loose cigarette or a quart of beer for himself. He loved his beer. And he would say "Thank you my girl". He always had a very heavy phlegmy cough, a bit of bad breath and the loveliest brown eyes. I loved them a lot. If I look back, I believed that I wasn't the best of the grandchildren, though I wasn't a child that demanded things. I appreciated the things I had. I was and always will be the black sheep of my family.

There was a time when I recall the lawyers sent a letter, and the aunt I had previously lived with, said I should say that my Nana was an alcoholic and I wasn't safe living at my maternal grandparents, due to him bringing his friends home etc.

Yes, he did drink, but I was told to bad-mouth them. And my heart still wanted to be with my aunt and her kids.

Today, I say that was actually wrong of me to side with her in doing that. My families always fought. It was like a never-ending story. Ma always got into arguments with her daughters because the fight was always about me. I think the fight wasn't actually who wanted to look after me, but who would take me in. I can picture this "no you take her, no I don't want her, you take her". Makes sense doesn't it? Children shouldn't be pushed around.

One day, I decided to run away. It was all just so annoying. I wished they would just send me to the orphanage and get done. I just could not handle all that drama. I felt like a reject doll. Not good enough to be part of a family.

On the days that I missed my cousins, Nana and I would walk to go see them. My Grandparents and Aunt did not live far from each other, about a kilometer's walk, using the short cut through the bush (veld/field). I was never to walk alone, I always walked with my Nana or Ma.

As time went on, my visits began to lessen. I didn't visit much because my aunt had hurt me so much. Something inside me said, "They don't really want you." Soon after I left my eldest aunts house, they started house renovations and buying brand new cars. Things that they couldn't do when I was there. They always never had enough money and now that I had moved out, there was a brand new BMW and brand new TOYOTA Corolla. My uncle resigned in that year that I had moved out, and they opened up their own hardware shop later on. I was happy that they were prospering in their life after I had moved out.

My heart cried out for the kids, but I just had to stay away. It was for my own good and sanity. That was the lesson of cutting ties with people. It hurt a huge amount. It was something I had to learn to do if I was going to live this life of pain. If this was a way to shield myself from the pain, then so be it. A foundation was laid down on the inside of me, remember if you build a strong foundation, your house will not fall apart. My first layer was applied, and it was the beginning of something I never knew would give me the strength for the future, for the days and years to come.

If being strong at this age was what I needed, then choosing to be strong it would be. I had to be strong and look out for myself. I held this pain in for my wellbeing. I never forgot how I was treated. It did cross my mind, and it is still something that plays on my mind. Maybe I was not meant to be there. I was that extra baggage.

My bonding time with my grandparents was now my priority. The thought of them passing away did scare me. Where would I go? Who would want an orphan?

Most importantly, I finally found motherly love. I never lacked the motherly affection around Ma! Ma filled that space I longed for. It was not empty hugs, fake smiles and half-hearted love. This was given whole.

Weeks went by and I soon settled in. Ma and I loved watching wrestling. Wednesday and Saturday Nights, if I remember clearly, was our wrestling night. We would clean up early and snuggle up in bed to watch our favorite wrestlers, wrestle it out.

Nana, however thought we were mad, because Ma and I would jump on the bed, scream and shout like the wrestlers could hear us through the TV. Nana said we were two mad things. At my grandparents' home, around the house was cemented. I can say it was a "stoep", yes, it did have red polish on it too. If that's what you were thinking.

This stoep had to be polished to maintain that red and its shine. I offered, one weekend, to assist polishing it. After all, it didn't look so hard. What on earth was I thinking? It was hard labor to be on my hands and knees polishing all the grime off the floor. Red polish was everywhere, including me. That stoep made me work! And obviously, Ma would come to inspect the job. Once the floor was polished, you had to let it dry. Nobody was allowed to walk on it because it would make "Red, red everywhere." After the drying phase, you needed to shine it! So, again on all fours, I made that stoep shine. That was the last time I offered to put polish and shine the stoep!

Ma and I slept in the same room. I was always scared to sleep alone. Ma was always warm and I would cuddle up to her. I felt safe. On one winter's night, I had the fright of my life. I actually cried.

It was very cold. Ma had these homemade Duvets; we called it a Gudree (pronounced as Good – Ree). When I mean heavy, trust me it is extremely heavy. It felt like you were carrying a ton.

Bear in mind, Ma didn't believe in heaters, so you had to stick to the old-school vibes.

So anyway, we went to sleep. This Gudree covered us and it kept us warm. It's the best homemade duvet to keep warm and if you want an awesome bed made on the floor, use a Gudree. We fell asleep, and in the middle of the night I wanted to cuddle. I felt so cold. Did I get a shock, Ma's body was ice cold! I thought I was sleeping next to a dead body. I woke up and put my finger by her nose to check if she was breathing. I shook her up! She responded by asking what had happened, because by this time I was crying my eyes out. So, I told her, that her body was ice cold and I thought she had died. She had a good laugh, and promised she would not leave me.

I was petrified of being left alone, especially after the traumatic experience of losing my entire family. What would I do if I was left again?

One evening, the electricity went off. I was busy doing my homework with my room door closed. And the next thing, I was sitting in darkness. Shew weee! Did I run out of that room. But, failing to realize that the door was closed and locked, I ran into the door, and in the process the key fell off. I had to search in the dark, unlock the door and get out. I stood outside until Ma got home.

It was always laughs with ma, we did have our misunderstandings, but I could never have the heart to be angry at them. When we were sick, Ma would massage us with an oil that consisted of camphor, cloves, mustard seeds and oil. It was heated a little on the stove and while it cooled off Ma would warm her hands on the heated stove plates, take a little oil and massage you at the stove. That massage, done by any mother relieves you of any sickness. Ma always played, laughed, danced, sang and did all my stupid requests. I wanted my hair to be purple, it was the in-thing to take Kungoo (Purple powder used in prayers) and put it in your hair. Ma was my guinea pig. Ma was always game to try my ideas. She tried her level best to make me happy. And I loved her so much and the same with my Nana.

Nana was just as lovable, he loved his gardening, and Ma had to lock up our room doors because Nana would take things to sell. That was when he needed beer or cigarette money. And when Ma noticed that something was missing, all hell broke loose. The one day, he got so drunk he fell and hurt himself. There was just always something. But living with them was special and fun. They loved each other so much, regardless of my Nana sometimes being abusive towards Ma. They truly loved each other. Nana would scream from his room; "Mum, Mum make my food hot" or "Mum I want to bath, take my clothes out".

Characters from another generation.

Ma would attend Sai service (We are devotees of our beloved Shri Sathya Sai Baba) and I would join in from time to time. Nana would accuse Ma of "going to see other men" and then the fight would start. I loved the temple service, it was always so peaceful and uplifting.

My grandparents tried their utmost to bring me up. They brought me up with good values and I will treasure that. They brought me up as they did their own children. The same rules applied, with tweaks now and then.

Ma would take me visiting or for holidays. Remember, we didn't have a car, and neither of us drove. There were times we got a lift with some family member or friends of Ma's that was going to wherever it was. Sometimes, Ma's nieces, nephews or children fetched us, and at other times, we took a taxi. It was nice to travel and visit everyone. My dad always did that every weekend.

Ma's youngest daughter lived in Kinross. She's the one who got married just before my parents' passing. Remember the wedding that we had a blast at? It was her wedding. We would sometimes go and visit her.

Ma lived a thrifty lifestyle, Ma saved where she could.
One day, another letter arrived. This time it wasn't good and it was basically a family decision. My grandparents were old, and just as I thought they could pass away at any time, the law feared that too, and was concerned that they were not able to assist with my school work.

A decision needed to be made, if someone in our family will adopt me or, would I go into the system and get adopted by total strangers. Ma was my legal guardian, even though I was left in those so-called capable hands of my aunt. I guess my aunt had lost that right the day she packed me up. Ma and Nana were frail, and I gathered that I would have to move again. This time, either into a family or an unknown person's home or into the system. Ma's brother offered to take me in, but for some reason, someone or Ma didn't agree. And once again, there were arguments. Saddened by this news, I once again thought of suicide, because I felt like my own blood just didn't want me. No one, except my grandparents. They had known the importance of bringing me up.

All this over and over again, I wondered if it was actually worth living.

I sometimes stole a cigarette or two from Nana's hidden stash to smoke. The smoking story happened when I was in Grade 8. My aunt's eldest daughter decided we should try it. Mind you, she was 2 years younger than I was. I tried it and never took a liking to it. My cousin on the other hand, liked it a lot. But sometimes that urge or stress pulled me towards a cigarette or two. I felt like my world had once again, crumbled. That dark place swallowed me and there was nobody to notice what the world was doing to me. What the adults in my life may have thought was fun, was actually torture.

When I was alone, I would think of ways to kill myself. Then I would think of Ma and Nana and what impact it would have on them. I recalled the day I hung over the four coffins, trying to wake my family from the dead. Was killing myself worth it? Was it worth causing pain to the handful of people that loved me? All these questions just kept on coming. Maybe everyone would be better off without me.

I would sleep more because that was where I found peace. It was a place where I could get away. A decision was made that I would live with my youngest Aunt. The one that lived in Kinross. And so, again, I was to be uprooted and moved to another home. I honestly felt like a tennis ball, being batted from one end to the other. I didn't have a choice. It was that or the orphanage.

This chapter ends here, the tales of living in Jozi. My Grade 10 year had come to an end and I had to start afresh, which meant new friends, new school and a new home. What was in store for me? Only the one I had faith in knew. Swami (Our beloved Shri Sathya Sai

Baba) knew what I was going through. Swami would get me through this. I was just hanging on.

It was sad to say goodbye to my friends that I had known for the three years of my high school life. On the last day of school, I remember collecting my report and I walked home. I walked home because I needed to clear my head. It was a long walk, my mind full of questions and tears running down my cheeks. A broken heart which never healed, each time it just broke into a million pieces.

It was fear, emotions and a lot more that ran through my head. Remember, Ma was old-school, and girls were not allowed to walk on the road. That, too, from school.

I arrived home and I started packing my things with an extremely heavy heart. What I had now called home would soon just become a memory, like my previous homes. Just history that people would read about, or learn that a child named Alicia Sewdass once lived here.

Was I just a name?
Was I just another child in the system?
Would I ever find my forever home?

I didn't blame my grandparents for this decision as it was not something they could have prevented or that they could have changed for me to stay with them.

I thought "How cruel is life?", "How does a child go from having a family of four, a loving home, to something so broken, something so painful." My heart ached and I wished that my parents would just pop out from somewhere and say that it was all just a joke and that reality could never be this cruel.

To my friends from Lenasia

Thank you, ladies, for always being there for me. The days when I needed to vent or just needed to talk, you were all there for me.
I never told you then, but those moments, those days you cried with me, the days you supported me, it meant the world to me. I will forever treasure the love and kindnooo you ɕhared with me

Thank you.

My dear reader, my friends played an important role in my high school years.

On the days that I needed to vent or I felt that I was crumbling on the inside, they stood by me and cheered me up. I started speaking more to my friends about things at home and my tragedy. I felt the more I spoke, the better I felt. They understood me, they never judged me. Even if they couldn't give me advice, just by having them listening to me vent made me feel better.

Some relationships happen for a reason or even just for a moment, and whatever the reason any of my friendships or relationships formed, I cherished them.

REFLECTION

Grandparents are a work of art, masterpieces that I wish could live forever. If there is one thing to learn from this chapter it would be to love, live and learn to forgive. We cross paths with millions of people in our lifetime, even if it's just for a second. I assure you there is a reason for you to meet them. Surround yourself with people that have a positive influence on you.

8

DATING GAME

I dated in Grade 8, and my first boyfriend was my childhood friend. It was something I was new to. I was never allowed to date while my parents were alive.

Mum caught me one day. I was in Grade 7 and I really liked this boy a lot and I felt that he should know about my feelings. I built up the courage to write him a letter.

In this letter, I disclosed my feelings. I then hid the letter under the blankets. Mum found it while cleaning.

Mum told me I was too young and when the time was right, she would tell me. Dad didn't know of this because then my head would be on a chopping block for such behavior.

In Grade 8, my eldest aunt allowed me to date. This boy had given me my first kiss, wrote me love letters and bought me gifts. He made me get butterflies in my tummy. It soon ended and I noticed other boys in school liked me too. A simple "Will you go out with me?" from a boy and myself saying "Yes", meant we were dating. I had a few boyfriends and I feel bad now because I know for some, I never had any feelings or liked them. My eldest cousin always called me "Ali

Baba and her 40 boyfriends" because the boys kept asking me out. They wanted to date me, they liked me and I was not interested. They'd buy me chocolates. I ate them and said no I can't date them. The attention felt good, but I didn't understand why they would want to date me. I was not as beautiful as most of my friends or other girls in the school. I mean, I was still very insecure, and I never liked the way I looked. I had extremely bushy eyebrows, a moustache and beard. I wasn't the most presentable or popular chick in school. I admired that the girls took pride in their hair and looks. I was just your plain Jane. My Uncle had once told me that there is no cure for ugliness. That always made me feel less attractive about myself. I believed his words.

In those days, I didn't tweeze, wax or thread my facial hairs. It never bothered me in the least about how I looked, or how I should look. Maybe tone down the brows or moustache so that the boys could like me more. It just never bothered me.

I admired the girls in my school that took time to groom themselves. Some girls had hairstyles for each day, they applied make-up and they were just so beautiful. We carried mirrors and hairbrushes, our famous Labello always stayed close by. "Lips love Labello".

I was very concerned about my teeth and breath, though, and to this day that is my first priority and then my facial hairs.

The boys that liked me were not from the popular group either. But for some reason, these guys liked me, or they made it look like they did. Boys sometimes just say they are dating girls just to run up scores on how many they have dated when they are amongst the

115

guys, and more importantly, I was still a virgin. I told myself I would only lose my virginity to the man I knew I would marry.

I treasured my virginity and to me it was sacred that I lose it to someone I love.

I had never forgotten what morals and values my parents had instilled in me, along with other life lessons and values I learnt after their death. My father's name, Sewdass, was important and I was not to ever drag that name through the mud.

At one point, I decided to cut my hair extremely short, just so that the boys would stop asking me to date them. That did not work, it just made it worse. Time went on and eventually I decided to stop dating and concentrate on my studies. You will hear more about that in the chapters to come. As the years went on, I felt I should start dating when I started to work in 2006. I was looking for love and finding that one soul to settle with. Someone who would accept me for who I am and never hurt me.

It seems like as you get older, people start hooking you up with guys and girls. Almost playing match maker. If it works, it works. If it doesn't, just move on.

There was a guy a friend of mine mentioned I should meet.
As nothing hurts trying, I agreed to chat to him over SMS and Mxit.

Upon our second meeting, I hadn't cleaned up well. Like I mentioned, grooming wasn't my strong point. My eyebrows were bushy and my upper lip hairs visible, while hugging and kissing him (I hated the

French kisses. I avoided those) he tells me, "Your facial hairs disgust me."

What?
Seriously, did he just say that?
Fine, I understand it's a put-off for the male species, but nobody is perfect.
I broke up with him straight after.
Hell no!
No ways am I going to hear rubbish like that.

Some boys were total mummy's boys, or they just wanted to have sex and I refused, which resulted in breakups. Good riddance! When I was 21, there was another boy, who was also referred to by a friend. He was a very nice, humble boy. We clicked and he was ready for marriage, but I felt I was still not ready.

The pressure came in from all sides. His mum mentioned I should call her mum, since they had already bought my sari for our proposal ceremony. Seriously!

The week this "meeting" was to happen, I ended up in hospital for a week whilst in Durban on holiday. Do you know that the guy did not visit me because he had a sore throat? Mind you, his mum had to call to say this to me while I was in hospital. To think that over the upcoming weekend, I was to meet his parents. Thank you Swami, that this popped up. As time went by, some aunty, you know, some auntie's must poke their noses in other people's business just because she wanted this boy for her daughter. This stranger aunty went and spread rumors to this boy's mother that I was not a nice girl and I had a man living with me. By now you should know me, I don't like lies. I prefer to be told the truth to my face, not behind my back.

I put up a fight for myself because I was innocent. The twisted story was a lie. Yes, I did have a man living with me. That man was my uncle (my mum's first cousin) he moved in with me when my adoptive parents moved to another province.

This relationship came to an end because, I was not going to be with a man that wouldn't stand up for me. A man that would listen to stories.

Then there is Schivan Ramdharee my hunk of a husband. Oh, this isn't going to be written in this chapter, he deserves a chapter of his own. I met my husband while in Grade 11, 2004. That is all for now!

REFLECTION

Hormones. I blame them. There is no need to change to be like the others. Just be you! When you find the right person, they will love you for you. Finding love is trial and error or love at first sight. Getting an education is important, everything else can come afterwards.

9

MOVING AGAIN

With all my clothes packed and ready to leave from my Grandparents in December 2002, I said goodbye to my friends that lived close by, and off from my Grandparents I went. The great move to Kinross.

It felt like an extremely long drive to get to this place. All you saw on the roadside was, cows, sheep and crops with mealies and soya.

It was about a 1.5-to-2-hour drive, give or take, from Johannesburg to Kinross. It took forever. Eventually, we arrived at my new home. I was surprised to notice that everyone was so excited. My youngest Aunt and her husband didn't have any children at that time. All their friends were excited that they now have a child. They made such a bold move to take me in and I was ever so grateful because that meant I hopefully didn't have to move again. It meant that I would have a home and a family that just might not simply give me away. I was to spend my December holidays here, and then in January, find a school to attend for my Grade 11 year. Ma was very emotional. We had built a bond that was so strong. My heart sank when they both had to leave for Johannesburg.

I found myself in new surroundings and I had to settle in again. It was a very different atmosphere.

I had my own room and this time around, I had to sleep alone. I missed Ma so much. Every night, I would hold a pillow for comfort. The storms in the Highveld were horrible, and the thunder scared me the most. I hated stormy days, especially now that I was sleeping alone.

I had to adjust according to my younger aunt and her husband's rules as well as make a lifestyle change. Weeks went by and I started to feel comfortable. It really was a good atmosphere. I felt at home.

My youngest aunt raised me as my Ma had raised her children. Living with Ma for those few months actually helped a lot because those rules set in. I was already in sync, so there wouldn't be a problem in adjusting to my aunts rules. I could have friends, but no boyfriends and so on. I respected that.

No going out with friends unless they came home or my younger aunt and husband had met them.

No cellphones. I never owned one, until later in the year when my eldest aunt bought me one because every child had a phone.

Time went by so quickly, and before you knew it, it was the start of the new term for school. During the first week, we ran around looking for a school that I could be placed in.

Eventually, we managed to get a school, in Secunda. It was 18km away from Kinross. I was grateful that my education could continue. I was to begin school in the second week. Basically, I had missed out on sports day and all the other activities. This school had their own school song! I don't remember any of my previous schools having one.

Bear in mind that I didn't know anyone from a bar of soap. Nobody knew me or my story. This schooling year started on a clean slate, and I was actually more concerned about who I would make friends with, as I hated the idea of being alone.

The first day of school started and yes, I was petrified.
My uncle dropped me off at school that morning. I had to find my way to the main office. This set off a trigger for me. When I was younger, the first day of school was always a big deal. Dad would take photos and it was just an exciting first day, every year.

I missed my dad at that point because even though I was old enough, it was still my first day of school and every first day of school, my dad would walk me in. I sat in the reception area, and a kind secretary assisted me. She took me to my class and from there it was entirely up to me on how this was going to go. I can't quite remember what class I was placed in, but I remember that I was scared. I did manage to make some friends over the next few days. I was glad that I was not alone.

Since the school was 18km away, and my aunt and uncle worked from 07:00 to 16:00 I had to take a bus to school and back home.

This was actually a mission for me. Even though this was my first day, I had to make sure I was on the right bus. Different scenarios played out in my head. If my parents were here, this would be a no-go or they would probably park somewhere and make sure I got onto the bus ok. But this time, there was no "red golf" waiting for me. As it is, my late parents stressed when I got onto a bus for my school excursions. Imagine this.

When the time came to catch the bus, I panicked because I didn't know which one to get on to. Luckily, I spotted our neighbor. She was my Senior, a Grade 12 learner. Spotting her put me at ease and knowing she was there made my life a little less stressful.

The bus was full, and I quickly found out that the seniors, which were the Grade 12's, filled up the back seat, and everyone else would just follow from the next grade. That obstacle was done and dusted. It was not my first time sitting on a bus. I had been for many school excursions. It was however, my first time traveling on a bus to school and back home.

Because the towns were far apart, I had to rely completely on the bus. I didn't dare walk home or walk to school as it was just too far. That thought just jumped out the window. The good thing was, I could catch up on sleep. The route was long, from Secunda to Kinross, and with the various stops, it took at least an hour. From my stop it was a long walk to the house. It was fun, walking with my neighbors.

In the morning we had to wait for the bus from 06:00, because anytime from then, the bus would appear.

Yes, there were times that we missed the bus, and we had to run to the next stop to make it on time. Fun times, I tell you.

I dreaded the Winters waiting for the Bus. If you thought Johannesburg was cold, then you haven't experienced Winter like this.

School was school. I made friends and our group of friends grew. I loved school.

At home things were going really well too, though we did have arguments now and then.

There was a little shop at the corner of the Mall. They always had such beautiful ornaments of fairies and dolphins. I was allowed to purchase one ornament whenever we stopped by. At home, we would display them in the display cabinet.

After school, I would make me something to eat, and I loved making fried chips. It was my favorite and staple diet. A pocket of potatoes never lasted long. I guess I ate them all up! After eating, I would snooze a bit and then begin my homework. As I would get done with my homework, my aunty and uncle would arrive home from work. They travelled together.

I never helped preparing supper or cleaning. I kept to myself and when I was called to eat supper that was the only time I left my room. After eating, I would help to clear up, watch some TV with my aunt and uncle and then I would go back to my room. That was my habit. Some days I just didn't feel sociable. In the mornings they left for work and I would have to make my lunch for school. Some mornings

I cried while making my lunch. My Ma always made sure I had lunch. I was so used to an elder/parent making my lunch.

Some days I just took butter bread and sprinkled sugar on it, or nothing at all. Sometimes my uncle made me lunch. I was grateful that time went into thinking of me. It was not that they refused to make me lunch, I guess I just had to become responsible enough to make my own. I felt like all was going well. Ma assisted me to get a grant from the government, which soon came through. I can't remember how much it was.

A few months had passed, and I was settled in, but then I started to notice similar changes to when I stayed with my eldest aunt.
Our shopping got less, I was told to contribute and to use my grant money to pay for board and lodging. I had to use some of it to pay my school fees and to buy my bus tickets. I write this with a heavy heart, because if my parents were alive, I wouldn't have had to pay for board and lodging, neither would they have asked me to pay for my school fees or transport to school. Once again, my heart had sunk to the bottom of my tummy.

Ma didn't like it either. Whenever we visited her in Johannesburg or she came to stay, Ma always snuck a few Rands into my hand. I hid it well. I learnt to hide it well from the days of staying with my eldest aunt. Being kids, adults always gave us money when they visited, out of generosity. My eldest aunt would ask for this money on some days and I would gladly give it to help out. She always said, "I will give it back to you when I have the money." That day never came. Even if I had to ask, I was given a mouth full. I used that money to buy toiletries I liked. Likewise, in my new home nobody ever knew, except for Ma and myself. It was our secret. Bless our Grandparents' souls.

I questioned myself. Was I dealing with the same thing again, just a different version? Apparently, this was to teach me to be responsible. I didn't mind paying for my usage, but it was a stab into my heart. None of my friends' parents charged them for board and lodging. I felt like I was a stranger all of a sudden. Like I was just placed there.

I did as I was told, though. On a monthly basis, I would pay my board and lodging fee, and pay my school fees. Was I a child or an adult? I couldn't make sense of it at all! I thought parents took care of their children and spoiled them. I felt I was to be punished and be taught a lesson for "killing my family". That's what my family said. Those deadly words came out in almost every conversation.

"You killed your family."

I didn't ask to stay with them, they had offered. Or was this a trial run to see if they could handle a child, because they didn't have any children yet?

I felt sorry for them because they had many failed pregnancies. I prayed that they would have a successful pregnancy at some point. My heart was still in the right place, regardless of my environment.

Was I the best suited child to these parents?
I went with the flow. My Uncle collected R5's, and every Friday he would bring me R5's. My Aunt never knew about this. It was also a secret.

My eyes lit up, as any child would.

I saved it for a rainy day. On the days that I didn't take lunch, I would buy from the school tuck shop and spoil my friends. They would sometimes buy me things and it was only fair that I gave back.

With my years of experience, I mastered the concept of "SAVING OF MONEY".

I didn't have a piggy-bank to store the coins in, so I would throw them onto the highest shelf, out of my reach. If I needed it, I would have to search!

I was given spending money every Friday, but it was kept to a minimum, due to children selling and buying drugs and people stealing money from children. My aunt and uncle had to worry about my safety as well.

When I lived in Johannesburg, I was robbed of my jewelry and money. Trust me, it isn't a nice feeling to be held at knife point. When I told the adults what had happened, I was told, "You were asking for it."

Saving the money really helped me because I knew there were always rainy days. And, if it was their birthday or a special occasion, I at least had money to buy my aunt and uncle a gift. I mean, that's what we did, Tasha, Shiven and myself. I loved putting a smile on a person's face. I always thought of the people around me first, before myself. I put everyone first, regardless of how I was treated. It felt ok to just put them first. To gain some sort of reward-based acceptance.

This is how I got by. My uncle and I became very close and he reminded me a lot of my dad, especially with gardening. That didn't sit too well with my aunt because, once again, I was told that I wanted to steal her husband. My aunt had also found out that my uncle used to give me all his R5 coins and he was told that he was spoiling me and that it should stop.

I couldn't find my place without family throwing harsh words. They had a group of friends. We visited them, and they visited us. You know the story of friends coming over. I loved staying over not because the lady's daughter was my age, but because I felt her mother's love. I used to stay over on weekends, usually from a Friday and then my aunt and uncle would pick me up on the Sunday. My aunt and uncle didn't like that we all cuddled and that this friend had sons.

I never saw anything wrong with cuddling and sitting on their lap or hugging. Yes, it was wrong because I was a young girl, and girls don't do that but during that time, I never saw or thought of it as being wrong. When I look back, I agree that what I did was wrong. It was shameful of me to sit on a young boy's lap.

Many times, while growing up, we get advice from our elders and being a teenager, you think you know everything, but truth be told, listen to what your elders tell you (though not everything), because later on when you are older, you realize why they said what they did. Sometimes, some things are said that are not realistic or are said with a lack of understanding, so not everything I took seriously. Elders can be wrong too.

My aunt always spoke to me about how a girl needed to be. I felt sorry for them because their parenting began with a teen, and it's not so easy bringing up a teen. It must have been hard.

I admit I wasn't the easiest of teens. Finding myself and speaking out caused problems beyond problems.

I know I was a rebel. I don't like rules. Talk to me and we can come to an understanding. I tried my level best as well though, and all I really wanted was to find comfort in a mother's love. One day, my aunt and uncle's friends moved away. I was heartbroken.

What I saw between this mother and daughter, I had wished that I could have had that sort of relationship with my aunt. They had mother-daughter outings, spa treatments, hair treatments done together. It was all down to the fine details of facial products and I just used soap on my pimple skin. I started feeling less worthy, less beautiful, less loved and an empty me.

Nobody took that time to look at me except for my friends. One of my dear friends would try to at least tweeze my eyebrows during our lunch breaks at school. I will share another embarrassing moment with you. My periods were pretty painful. When I mean painful, I don't mean pain that is bearable, I bled extremely heavily, and on days that it was "that time of the month" I would call my uncle to fetch me from school. Standing and sitting was unbearable. Soon that became an inconvenience for my uncle, because he couldn't leave work early every "one day in the month". So, I would go to school with pain killers in my pocket and if I was sleepy from the dose, I would sleep it off in class, lunch breaks or in the sick bay.

The one day I bled so heavy that I actually messed myself. My best friend at that time, who is still more of a sister than a friend to me and currently lives 8 minutes away from me, came through for me in a real and wonderful way. It was the last subject for the day, English, then the bell sounded for the day to end, and it was time to go home. I had a wet, uncomfortable feeling, so I asked my friend to just wait with me until the rest of the class had left. I moved a bit off my chair and to my dismay, it was messed with blood. Oh, dear me, that meant my school pants were drenched in blood. My eyes filled up with tears and my friend could see the panic. We waited for everyone to leave. I stood up and I asked her to check my "bum area". As I had feared, it was soiled and was really bad. Our English teacher at that time was concerned as to why we were not moving. I blurted out "Madam, I have messed the chair, I am on my period and I am messed." I needed to clean the chair. Quick thinking from Madam and my friend, Madam handed me a bottle of water and we had tissues. My friend stayed with me. After cleaning up, I had to rush as I'd miss the bus if I was any later. My friend told me to tie my jacket around my waist so I could block the soiled bit of my pants drenched in blood. My friend offered that I go home with her to change, but I had to get home to sort myself out. By this time, I was so uncomfortable and pretty weary not to let my soiled bits show. I sat uncomfortably in the bus trying not to move too much as I may cause more parts of my pants to be messed. I dreaded the walk down my street it was a long 500m to home. I got home, showered and hand-washed all my clothing. That day it was such an embarrassing moment in my life, and since that day, my friend has never uttered this to anyone. That is one of the reasons why she is, and will always be, a special friend in my life. Thank you, Losh!

How I admired and loved being loved and cared for when I was in my friends' presence. I think there must have been something severely wrong with me, growing up. I admit, I did do wrong things, and I learnt from them, but I didn't ask not to be loved by a mother.

My heart hurt so much, yet at the same time, I had a warm smile to return. Wearing these masks became a part of me.

But I made another mistake. One that changed everything again. I think it was after my first term at my new school. We received my report and I had performed poorly and had bad results. With no warning, I was sent back to my grandparents' home. All my things packed. Lock stock and barrel.

At this point, I seriously wished I could die. I wanted to die so badly. Once again nobody wanted me. They stabbed the words at me: "If you don't straighten up, we will leave you here to stay with Ma". "We are leaving you by Ma to think about what you have done".

You know when you squash a piece of paper, then you pull it out and try to make it new? Those creases you caused don't ever go away, not even if you try to iron them away. The creases stay there!

If I could wear all those words, the mental and emotional abuse on my body, would you see how damaged I was?

I was almost like a reject doll, waiting to be loved. Just because Suicide took my family. Just because my father went ahead with his murder-suicide.

So, I went back to Johannesburg, to my Ma's house. I stayed there for the school holidays. I needed to think about what I had done. Ma and I spoke a lot. All I could see in her eyes was the sorrow and heartbreak she felt for me. Tears just rolled down her face. Every family has their issues, and we all have our place and relationship, good or bad, within our family, but I was just, I was just kept aside.

Everyone else seemed to love being with their family and children, and then there was me. My reality was miles apart from those around me.

I felt very alone. I felt utterly sad. I didn't ask to be left behind, I didn't ask to be an orphan. All I wanted was that love.
That four-letter word that messes us around so much. *Love...* I wanted that.

I was dying on the inside for love. I cried, day in and day out. I kept asking questions to Swami.

Why didn't anyone love me?
Was the problem me?
Was I such a terrible child that I had to be hated?
Maybe it was true, and I did kill my family and that was why everyone hated me. This was my punishment.

My days were clearly numbered, bright red in my head. I decided that if the change needed to happen, it would have to start with me. I was the wrong one in all of this, so I agreed to do better, and try my level best to not be a rebel. I was so sorry for everything. Everything was my fault and I would try harder. On the other hand, I couldn't take things lying down. I would still stand my ground if I was right. I didn't like being accused of things I didn't do or say. When that happened, I would still stand up for myself. I wouldn't be pushed around. Left is left and right is right.

When you are accused so many times of something you didn't do, it becomes the norm to just submit and say, "yes, I did do it" to maintain the peace! I on the other hand, was the opposite. I would fight for myself when I was right.

Ma made the call to Kinross to tell them I would change. I packed all my things. When I say all my things, it wasn't a bag of clothing needed for a week or two, it was everything I owned. Off I went to Kinross again.

Back at school, I tried to focus. I tried to get help from other learners. Time went by and I think I coped.

Things at home, though, didn't go too well.
My youngest aunt and I never got along. Part of me thinks that it is because of my eldest aunt stuffing rubbish into my younger aunt's head, or they both saw me as a real brat of a child. In most cases, I remember being told I was a terrible niece. My younger aunt always bought really nice things for my eldest aunt's daughter. Whatever that child asked for she got. Questions went off in my head from time to time.

Why?
Why must she get all the nice things? She has parents!
Why can't her parents buy that for her?

If I questioned this aloud, it was such an issue. My youngest aunt's response was that she had raised her when she was a baby and that they had that connection. My cousin was the favorite niece and apparently the favorite grandchild. My life took a backseat and I just had to watch as my heart broke. It dampened my spirits because, to me, it was wrong.

I didn't get spoilt, but she did. You know that saying, "Just bite your lip"? So, I tried to not fight back, to maintain the peace.

The one day, we were all at home and my younger aunt said something to me. I didn't like it. She was standing in the prayer room getting ready to pray.

I felt I was being attacked.

All I remember saying was, "You're standing there and praying. Do you want to know why God hasn't given you a baby yet? It's because you cannot look after me. One day, when you can, maybe then God will."

I stormed out to my room and stayed there.

Silence for days.
Uncomfortable because I might get kicked out.
I secretly packed for just in case.
My uncle finally addressed the elephant in the room he said that I should speak to my aunt with respect, as that was his wife and I had no right to speak to her like that. I know what I said came from the bus load of emotions I held back.

Was I really to blame?
Did that need to be said?

I went and I apologized, though I know it wasn't a wholehearted apology because I meant what I said. Things used to happen and I felt that my mum's family just despised me in every way. I was such a reject, a waste to be alive. I was called stupid, ugly, useless and I called myself that too.

Again, I just wanted to be treated like a child that had parents, not as an orphan. I feel that orphans are often used as tools. Oh, we will adopt you and then once the deed is done, we won't need you, or "when we fall pregnant." I know of orphans that got taken in and once their adoptive parents fell pregnant, that child was no longer needed to fill that empty space in their lives.

Time went on and on one occasion, we took a drive to visit my eldest aunt. My youngest aunt and uncle thought I was old enough, I could bring home some of my late parent's belongings.

To our surprise, when they had approached my eldest aunt with the suggestion, she said over her dead body would I get my parents' things. My aunt and uncle fought with her. They asked her how she could refuse to give me what was rightfully mine. What rightfully belonged to me! She just refused to give me anything.

We walked out empty handed that day, my heart once again sore.

Months passed by and we heard that my eldest aunt and uncle suffered a great loss. I felt bad for my cousins that had to suffer. It was winter and their house had burnt down.

Everything that belonged to my late parents burnt as well.
I sat and thought to myself, first you deny me my right to my parents' things to a point that I have nothing but in just one blow your entire house ended up in flames. Now you don't have anything. They say what goes around comes around and that was just the Universe sending back what you sent out.

Call me evil, but I laughed deep within myself. I felt that cold and emotionless feeling on the inside. Obviously, I could not display my excitement on the outside.

We truly felt really bad for them and decided to send them clothing and some extra household goods. Remember I mentioned that my clothes were packed in bin packets the day I was sent to my grandparents? The day I packed clothing that I decided to donate, ended up being packed in bin bags too. After some time, I realized, that through all the hurt and pain I experienced, someone from above had been watching. Someone had taken note of all my pain and suffering. They say karma is a bitch, and it's true. What goes around comes around.

REFLECTION

Life is full of surprises, what we take from it, is up to us.
How you interpret the situation is entirely up to you. Love not for the
sake of loving but loving from the heart because you mean every
ounce of that affection.

10

SCHOOL LIFE

I went on with school, and when I turned 16, I wished, like every other girl, to have a sweet 16 party. I got a sweet 16 pendant, which I loved, and I was forever grateful for that. It was the thought that counted, but deep down I planned an amazing 16th birthday party. I hoped that there was actually a surprise birthday party coming. I had high expectations for everything and it always ended up being a disappointment. It hurt again when no party came about but hey, this hurt thing was on repeat, so I guess I was good!

Special occasions messed me up emotionally.
The results for the last term were soon to be shared, and the term was coming to an end.

School ended and I received my report. Guess what??? *I had failed Grade 11.* I failed, I failed, and I failed! That's all I heard in my head.
I dreaded going home. I wanted to walk into an oncoming bus.
What was going to happen?
Was I going to be shipped off again?
I had never failed in my life. If my father was alive to see that moment, he would have been furious.

I had failed. It was done. All my friends had passed and were going to Grade 12.

I was embarrassed. I just wanted to hide, and I wanted to kill myself because I probably didn't have a home after this. The fear of going home was too real. I needed to die. All I did was crawl up into a little ball and be invisible until my aunt and uncle got home.

To kill myself or not was the question. In those gruelling few hours, I think I died a million times. I could have hanged myself under the carport, it was high enough a sari would be perfect. I could have run away. Many, many things went through my mind. I had even placed the chair under the carport to go ahead with my suicide. Nobody cared to ask if I was ok. Nobody cared if I lived. It was definitely better to be dead than alive.

They got home and I gave them my report.
They were furious as any parent would be, and I got shouted at.
Yes, I was wrong. So, I accepted my punishment and a few days later I was back in Johannesburg with my Ma. Every problem they had with me I was just sent back, like a reject item from store. "Hello, can we have a refund for the child, please? She did something wrong. She failed Grade 11."

The argument this time was if they should keep me or not. I had wasted a year and they were embarrassed that I didn't pass. I was at fault for my failure. I took full responsibility for that.

Then it was "what will people think?" and "Maybe she should just drop out of school and work." "On the point of work, who will hire a school drop-out or someone her age?" The words flew out like flying arrows.

I know I did try, but at the same time, I had not taken this schooling year as seriously as I should have. This school was on a totally different level compared to my previous school, and it should have been taken into consideration all the moving up and down between homes. But I was sorry.

From a parent's perspective, I had not done enough, because I did not pass. I never achieved that A.
You never got that Pass!
In my mind, I felt that I should have tried harder, I should have asked for help.
It was my fault I had failed. It was my fault alone. I beat myself up on the inside for messing up. I was scared that I may not be able to go back to school.
I had messed up my future!

So many things went through my head. The only comfort I had was my loneliness and my pillow that soaked up all my tears.
There was nothing I could do to rectify the "fail".
I thought I was so far messed up, that I would probably just kill myself, which was the better option. It was another school holiday, and more time to reflect on my life. I missed the days when we three went on holidays to the Drakensburg. It made me laugh. I cried because I was happy with them but they were not happy with me.

In everyone's eyes I was a failure, a let-down.

I was unhappy with myself because I tried to please and make everyone except myself, happy. I went against every rule in the book that my father had laid out. I didn't deserve to live.

I believed I was ugly.
I believed I was so stupid that I failed.
I believed I was dumb.
Nobody loves broken ornaments, you either throw them away or buy a new one.

What was I?
Who was I?

As the days went by something ignited from within me. This inner voice started speaking to me. My fighting spirit from within challenged me to go back to school. To prove every human being wrong and to turn my life into a success. Swear at me, hurt me, throw me out to the wolves, I don't care.

This new fire began raging on the inside of me not to give up and to show everyone how wrong they are. I decided to face my ghosts and go back to school. It was better to go back to school. I was a bit ashamed but hey, second chances are good.

In the year 2004 I went full on, in getting a pass in my Grade 11 year.

While prepping to go back to school, we went to Durban for a small holiday. It happened again, even with my different attitude. While shopping, we had my uncle's niece with us, and we went together to shop. She was allowed to choose whatever clothing she liked, and when I asked if I could choose as well, I got told, "You have to choose between school clothes or casual clothes. You are going back to school, so decide if you want to wear old school clothes."

I shut my mouth held back my tears and watched. I chose school clothes. I had outgrown my shirts and pants. I would not want to be seen with short clothing.

I walked behind them all the way. They looked so happy with other people's children but not with me.

The first term arrived and I was ready to kick ass, more especially I had promised myself to prove everyone wrong and I vowed to work to buy the things that nobody else could provide for me.

During this year of schooling, I wasn't allowed to go out with friends. No movies, no suppers, no sleepovers, no school balls, nothing. It was not like I got to go for any of these in my previous year so, I knew the rules. Whenever a friend would ask me out to go ten pin bowling or for a movie, I always made something up and the answer was always no. I wished I could attend my school functions but, because of the answer always being no, it was the norm to just tell myself no.

By not asking, it made me a good child, because I never asked to meet with friends, to go out or to go to the Valentine's day dance or Spring dance. I never knew what it was like to attend a dance. I did have crushes, guys that I liked, that didn't like me. That was life. I grew a set of balls and got over it. Somehow in my second year of Grade 11, it really didn't bother me much if I fitted in or had a boyfriend. I had a challenge, a challenge to prove to everyone that even though you may fail, you can pass.

I became more involved in our Sai group. I attended temple, I started believing in God again, more in Swami, the one I truly have faith in. If Swami got me this far in life, surely there has to be some good in it. My spiritual side started to develop. During the year of 2004 my aunt and uncle started to loosen up and allowed sleepovers at my friends' homes. They were friends from our temple group.

This in a way, also helped me to just get away from home sometimes. It was still a thick atmosphere on certain days.

I paid more attention in school. I went for tuitions, and my new group of friends helped me a lot. I was terrible at Mathematics, English, and Afrikaans.

My uncle would sit with me every night and teach me mathematics, and we played scrabble as a family to better my English. I watched 7de Laan, to perfect my Afrikaans however I did cheat a bit and get a friend to do my Afrikaans speeches. My aunt and uncle were actually more involved in my school work than in my first year of Grade 11. Things went much better at home. I think by then they had put in an application to legally adopt me. I was finally officially adopted, and the days of moving from house to house were over, or so I hoped.

There were some days that I didn't wish to go home, and I jumped off at a friend's house. His mum was really so sweet and I would ask for advice from her. Before my adoptive parents could get back, I would be home. I did do things I wasn't allowed to do. I did them and never said a word. I just needed to know if what I was experiencing was normal.

My life had changed. I found a group of friends at school that I simply adored, some of whom I still hold close to my heart. We were easily 15 in this group. We copied homework in the mornings, and sometimes we just helped out where we could. If you were good in this subject, you helped out. Birthdays were a big deal in our group and we loved free classes.

Well, the year came to an end. Term 4 ended and it was time for the results. I had done it. I passed extremely well and was going to Grade 12! Whoop! The excitement, the celebrations. Oh yes, I couldn't attend those because I would be told no. I made an excuse to my friends.

This was the first December that I could remember not being shipped off.

I was extremely happy to be in Grade 12, and a senior. This meant I got to sit at the back of the bus. We were seniors at school. It was our final year of school, and we all had this "we can do this" attitude.

During the year 2005, it was Mother's Day when we found out my adoptive mum was pregnant. Or should I say, *I* found out, while we had visitors over. It came as a shock to me that I wasn't told personally. I found out that they were pregnant when they mentioned it to the people visiting.

I was excited for them but at the same time sad. Sad that they didn't tell me and sad that they might ship me off again. I was excited and over the moon that I may have a sister or brother, if they kept me. I prayed that it went well. They had so many failed pregnancies, I prayed to Swami, that this pregnancy be full term and to let this one be perfect.

My adoptive mum started to show and a little belly was developing, I got to go for one of her check-ups and I heard the baby's heartbeat. I really couldn't wait. The excitement was building up, while I felt my life starting to break again.

Now, you do know that a Matric farewell ball is what everyone waits for. I think my grades where bad or they found this ball to be a distraction, I can't quite remember what it was, but my adoptive parents refused to let me attend.

My world shattered again. Why? Everyone was going!

It was our matric ball. My Ma stepped into the picture to beg and plead, that they send me. My teachers also grew concerned and tried to speak to them. Eventually my adoptive parents decided to send me, but alone with no partner. Oh well, at least I was going, A week before the Matric ball, I got my dress. Ma took me shopping for the perfect dress. Girls were talking about make-up trials and nails and hairdos. I sat there like this was really a big affair and I was just walking in. Well, all that was arranged for me, with a dear friend of my adoptive parents. She did my hair and makeup and I was ready to go. A close friend of ours arranged a car for me, he was like a brother to me. He escorted me out the car and into the hall. On our way in, my Afrikaans teacher asked him if he was my partner for the night. We explained that I was alone. She said not to worry, that she had paid for him already. My angel in disguise, Thank you Madam. That day, you made a girl's dream come true. The night was perfect, and I enjoyed it.

Trials approached soon after, and my adoptive mum was once again moody with me and my adoptive dad. It was her 3rd trimester and her hormones were raging beyond crazy.

During my trials, she threatened to take all my books and burn them. I think it was the hormones from the pregnancy, but this was still on so many levels of wrong. The one day, I found all my books scattered in the tub. She was going to fill the tub with water to soak them!

I was in my final year, I was about to write the most important exams of my life, and she wanted to destroy my books. The one day, she dragged me outside and hit me. Apparently, I spoke badly about her to a family member and everyone thought she was mad. I raised my hand to defend myself.

I was then accused of trying to hit her and harm her unborn child. I think it must have been all her hormones. I really didn't take anything to heart. If she had only known how much love I had for her and her unborn child. I would rather put myself in harm's way to protect them. Nobody to this day knows how much love I have to give. Not even my husband.

This was now getting completely out of hand. My adoptive dad decided that I should move all my books to his friend's flat, and every morning he would drop me off there. That way, I could study and go write my exams. Since my adoptive dad's friends flat was close to school, I could walk to school. This went on until final exams.

During all this drama and preparation for my final exams, I planned my adoptive mum's baby shower with a few ladies from our community and temple group. I did the décor and everyone brought little eats and gifts. I know my adoptive mum couldn't stand the sight of me. During the baby shower, I just stayed in the shadows. A simple thank you would have been nice. Instead, I had received cold, dagger looks. She hated me, and this time I am sure it was not the hormones. It was pure dislike and hatred that she felt towards me. I let it be and cried it out when I was alone. It hurt so badly. I didn't deserve this.

On the day of our last exam, our group of friends decided to go paint ball shooting. And me? Well, obviously you would know my story by now. No. This time I decided I would lie and go out with my friends, because some of them knew why I made up excuses. Together, we made a safe plan and I lied to my adoptive parents and went paint ball shooting. Oh man, was it fun! I came back, black and blue, and it hurt but hey, I had never lied to get out before and this was the last time I would probably see my friends. I hate lying. I can't lie, and if I do, it's probably a white lie!

The Grade 12 results were out and I was stressed out and panicked. My adoptive dad poured a stiff shot, which I downed, to calm down. Once I had calmed down, we bought the newspaper and I went through it and I had passed! To add to the joy, my adoptive mum gave birth to a beautiful baby girl that December.

That brings me to the end of my schooling days… But not quite. I did mention previously that I met my Husband in Grade 11.

Yes, there is more heartache and drama to add to this story.

REFLECTION

Failure is a stepping stone in life it's not the end. Your life shouldn't end because you've failed. The most successful people have failed. They didn't give up instead they used it, to see how they can do it better. Parents, normalize that is okay to talk openly about suicide awareness and mental health issues. No child should feel that taking their life is okay! A child should be able to come to discuss anything and everything with you as a parent. Believe in your child, encourage them to do well, create positive self-talk. Remember what is traumatic for one may not be for the other person. Not everyone's trauma is the same!

11

FINDING LOVE

In my second year of Grade 11, 2004, I met my darling husband, Schivan. The way we met was quite extraordinary, read on there's more heartache.

Dating in my era was different to the dating in my adoptive parent's era. But none the less, I dated as I did when I lived in Johannesburg.

For me, if a guy had asked you out in school, it made you boyfriend and girlfriend and you dated.

With my adoptive parents, I would have to bring the boy home so they can get to know him and so forth.

I never could understand why! Why bring him home if you were just dating? I mean, it was not like I was going to marry him. As time went on, I dated secretly. Obviously I was not allowed to go to movies or suppers. I couldn't even think of asking "Can I go out with my friends?"

Ten million questions would pour out.
Who are your friends?

We don't know them.
Who are their parents?

So rather not ask! That was the rule in my brain. I understand that there was a reason for this. My safety was a priority.

I started to get more involved in my spiritual paths, going to temple, learning the teaching of Sri Sathya Sai Baba and doing seva (service to mankind). I loved listening to the bhajans (devotional songs) that were sung in temple. It just took me to another level. We hosted our first medical camp at one of our communities. This medical camp offered free services to the people living in this community. A lot of hard work had been put into making it a success and it was. The day arrived and we prayed for blessings that our function would go well. It was on this day that I met my love.

Call me a bit too much, or a hopeless romantic, but the night before, I had wished on a shooting star and prayed to Swami to send me someone that I could call mine. I know, I was too young to think of a steady boyfriend at the age of 17, but I wanted that. A friend and I were doing the admin of all the patients that day. It was mid-winter. As I was doing my admin, I noticed a really tall guy from afar. He was handsome and tall. It was like he stood out from the crowd. So, I asked my friend who that boy was, as I had never seen him before. She told me he was from the Standerton Sai Centre. "Oh, I see.", I responded.

Time went on and I needed a cup of coffee to warm myself up. I left my station and made my way to the kitchen. I noticed that this tall boy was staring at me like crazy. Every time I turned around, I caught his gaze. He was the photographer for that day. I named him "Camera boy".

I got to the kitchen and scouted around for some snacks as the kettle water started to boil. I made my coffee and was ready to go back to assist. To my surprise, this Camera boy walked into the kitchen. And now I got to check him out properly. I sized him up, from head to toe. His eyes made me weak and my heart just pounded as he gradually walked up to me. The nerve of this Camera boy, he did not even introduce himself, all he did was stare! How rude!

All of a sudden, these words came flying out of his mouth.

He just blurted out:
"Will you make me a cup of coffee, please?"
Oh my word, I hate making tea and coffee for others. I just can't, especially while caught off guard like this, by the tall, handsome Camera boy.
I responded in my most straightforward tone:
"You've got hands, you've got legs, make it yourself!"
Was I over-cheeky?
Well, he had it coming!
I was not going to be making coffee for him!

The day went by, and the stares and bumping into each other kept on happening. My tummy felt tickly and I felt so drawn to his stares. My knees jolted every time!
That evening, our medical camp had come to a close. It was time to clean up and serve supper to all our guests that assisted in making this medical camp such a success.

After the clean-up, my friend finally introduced us.
"Schivan! This is Alicia". "Alicia, Schivan."
"Nice to meet you, Coffee girl."
"Hmmm, nice to meet you, Camera boy!"

We later exchanged cell phone numbers at the temple. It was weird, because I didn't look like girlfriend material. There were prettier girls around. I never knew what boys my age would look for in a girl, I mean, at just 17 years old, some of us were still so immature.

Night fell and everyone parted ways. He said, he would call me. I went home thinking he was just another guy and I was sure he wouldn't call me. I mean why would he? I didn't look pretty at all!

The next day at school I shared my juicy "meet and greet" with my girls, and I felt so happy about everything. Night came and went. Another day gone by and no calls, no messages. Oh well, I guess he decided not to call me.

A week later, and BOOM! This person sends a message. It was Schivan, from temple. I kept spelling his name wrong and he kept correcting me. We chatted over SMS and Mxit at that time. We enjoyed chatting to each other. I can't remember our conversations, but it was different in every way. Our chatting went on until I met him again for Swami's birthday, in Standerton. I was nervous because it had been months of us chatting and being friends. Swami's birthday was done beautifully, and it was time to head back to Kinross. Before leaving, he told me that he really liked me and asked me to be his girlfriend! I was shocked, as much as I wanted it. Wow! A boy likes me! He told me I had until midnight to give him an answer. No pressure here! Well, I obviously knew my answer would be YES!

And so it began. We called it dating, but hardly saw each other. Neither of our parents knew. We would secretly call each other when everyone was asleep. We would whisper our conversations so nobody heard us. He would send me airtime. His parents owned a shop, so I guess that's where some of your airtime went to, Uncle J! There was not a day we didn't speak. If I didn't have airtime, I would send him a Please-Call-Me, and vice versa. We met only at temple functions and obviously had to be very discreet. No first kiss or holding hands happened, until we had our Unity of Faiths rally. I got to sit next to him and he held my hand. If my heart could have jumped out of my chest and dance on the stage, it would have!

After a while, I think our parents knew something was up. On Valentine's day he gifted me a pair of earrings. It was my first ever *real* Valentine's day gift. I got him some basket thing. That too, was very discreetly exchanged at the temple. I wore those earrings with pride and happiness.

Since we were still in school, and now in our final year of schooling, my adoptive parents felt that I was not performing well and took away my phone and I was not to have any contact with Schivan.

I was told to end everything. My world crumbled again. I respected it and did what I was told, but we couldn't be without each other. I had memorized his number and I would SMS him from a friend's phone in school or go to the pay phone on the corner of our street. Yes, I did do all that behind the backs of my adoptive parents.

One night, I decided to go looking for my phone while they were out. I found it in the cubby of our Nissan champ. Yes! I was back in the game but I only had access to the phone when my adoptive parents were not around.

We needed to make a decision about *us*, because we couldn't go on like this. Some friends of my adoptive parents had informed them that Schivan's family was not a good family. They told them all sorts of back-in-the-day stories from Newcastle. I was then told to not even look at him or smile at him. That was harsh, and it hurt because my adoptive parents believed the stories from others, instead of getting to know him as an individual.

Time went by, and there was another function at the temple. We decided to meet there and maybe talk. I was already seated when he arrived. As he walked through that door, my bells went off and I smiled. My adoptive mum immediately sent me home. That felt like the worst thing she could have done, and I decided to use my phone and sent him a Please-Call-Me. He called back.

I told him he could come home, that I was alone, and at least we would have time together to discuss our relationship.
Little did I know, the drama had only just begun.

Schivan and his accomplices made some story up so they could leave temple with Schivan. They had Schivan's dads' van. They dropped him off at my house and drove off.
Oh, the relief that we could finally talk under no red tape. We had just started talking when his phone rang. His friends told him my adoptive

parents were on their way towards my home. I completely panicked, because I knew that I had broken a rule by inviting him over without my adoptive parents at home. I opened the gate and we had to find the quickest way for him to go out. Stupid me, instead of telling him to jump the fence, I opened the driveway gate and told him to go out there. But stupid him, he could have stayed as well. We were both in deep trouble for this. As he ran out, my adoptive parents had reached the 3rd house from us, and saw him running. Oh, man. Now all the demons were out and I had to bear the brunt of it all. This needed an explanation, and I gave it honestly. I included how I found my phone. My phone was now gone for good and I was grounded. I could not even go to the temple.

My adoptive parents were fuming with anger. I don't blame them. I was wrong. Schivan and I were wrong, but, in a way, it felt unfair to not allow me to smile or speak to him. Our dating language and their dating language was so different. They had made their way back to the temple and I am sure by then the entire Sai center knew what had transpired. Well, I am sure you pieced things together that someone had overheard what Schivan and his friends planned and told my adoptive parents. Thank you to that wonderful soul.

The scene played out at temple over lunch. There are two versions of stories that I have heard. One, from my adoptive parents and, later on, the one from Schivan. (we did meet again!)

My adoptive parents told me that they addressed Schivan's dad, and that we were not to have any contact with each other. I needed to concentrate on my school work, and this was a huge distraction.

Apparently his dad's response was, "You take care of your shit and I will take care of mine!" For the time being, this was the only story I had heard until Schivan shared his side, years later.

My response to them was that I was not there to witness the words exchanged between both parties. I would not believe anything I did not hear. Even now, I will not side with anything that was said on that day because I was not present. At 17, I learnt that stories get twisted, the truth gets lost in translation and if you didn't hear and see it with your own eyes and ears, don't believe it!

I missed him so much. I couldn't fall asleep, because I had gotten so used to hearing his voice before I slept, and to hearing the words, "I love you." Days went by I cried endlessly. I had been happy and yet again, it was taken from me. Was I never going to be happy? Was I always supposed to listen to others?

On nights alone at home, I would walk outside to our carport. I would look at the beams and think of how I should hang myself. How would I tie the sari onto the beam. I'd place the chair and the sari and measure out, just so my attempt wouldn't fail. Now, more than ever, I needed care. I became distant in many ways. I just focused on my schoolwork and wore that well selected mask of "she is well", but deep down, I was drowning and I could not stay afloat. I didn't even speak to my adoptive parents about my thoughts and feelings and it didn't seem important to let anyone know what was going on in my head. I struggled.

Because of my drama episode, I was no longer allowed to be home alone. After school, the bus had to drop me off on the other side of town and I spent my day with close friends of my adoptive parents. To this amazing family that stepped in to look after this damaged teen, thank you for your warm hospitality and love. You will never know how much that meant to me. Through spending time at your home, I had less time to plot my suicide.

I felt that nobody needed me. If nobody could even take the time to ask me how my day at school was, then surely my life didn't matter. I don't remember ever being asked that by my adoptive parents, and that's something for another chapter.

Our Grade 12 results were released and I secretly checked that Schivan had passed. I was happy that he had made it. I know he had plans to study further at the University of Johannesburg. During our "No Communication" phase, my adoptive parents gave back my phone and I would always type out messages to him and delete them. I didn't want a repeat of drama. I would get hidden caller ID calls, but as soon as I would answer, the person on the other end would cut them. Some part of me always knew it was Camera Boy. Every night before I fell asleep, I always said a silent "I love you." Whether it mattered or not, I still said it!

The following year, he went to University and I focused on myself. We went our separate ways. In the years to come since 2005, there was always an occasional Sai function that made us bump into each other. It was like a scene from a Bollywood movie. How these two souls just pined to be with each other. I'll stop here because there are more parts. So just keep this love story in mind.

In the years to come, even if Schivan or his parents greeted my adoptive parents, my adoptive parents ignored them completely.
I felt so bad because nothing is wrong in greeting a person. I always greeted back.

REFLECTION

Regardless of how it happens, there will be heartbreak. Relationships do end but that should not be the reason to end your life! Focus on building yourself up. If it's meant to be, it will be.

12

BECOMING MISS INDEPENDENT

After school, I had no idea what I wanted to study. I didn't have funds to study further, so I assisted my adoptive mother in looking after her baby girl. My adoptive mother's maternity leave was coming to an end. Since I was not working, I offered to look after her baby. I really didn't mind because I had looked after my brother and sister, and when I stayed with my eldest aunt, I took care of my cousins, so I knew I could do this. Besides, we were living under the same roof.

Yes, there were people who threw in their 10 cent comments that I should find a job. That work would not just fall in my lap, etc. Dear people, if only you knew how hard I had tried.

My first job was in a video shop. I worked Monday to Sunday. It was okay, until the owner asked me if I play with myself. I felt so uncomfortable that I left. I told my adoptive parents that this was what the man had asked me and I told them I didn't ever want to go back.

My adoptive parents always introduced me as their eldest daughter, but I could not bring myself to call my youngest aunt and uncle "mum and dad". I referred to them as my adoptive parents and I continued to call them as taught when I was a child. Mosi means mothers sister and Mosa is what I would call her husband. So, it stayed that way "Mosi and Mosa" and not "mum and dad".

I may have had so many issues growing up as a teen, but they raised me as their own.

My adoptive mum had to go back to work and the baby was only 3 months old. I was 19 at that time. I went head on in looking after this miracle baby. I loved her so much. I took care of her as if she was my own. Diaper changes, bathing her, feeding, trying to catch up on sleep whenever she slept. So, for the people that keep telling me, I should learn how to look after a baby, I did that when I was 19 years old! When baby got sick, my adoptive mum and I would take turns going to the hospital. I would do the day shift, and my adoptive mum did the night shift. She would sleep over at the hospital. I would go home to rest and come to the hospital the next morning with my adoptive dad. I gave it my all. This child grew so fond of me I was her world, and she was mine. She still is.

In August 2006, I received the good news that I had got a job at a reputable company. I was ecstatic, because very few people had faith in me. Many wished the worst. I was blessed to have started my career in a petrochemical company in Secunda. I ended up working in my dream company and remained there for 8 years. My life was set. I had an income, and I still helped out in my adoptive parents' home, just as I had done before.

Unfortunately for my baby sister, she had to attend day care, as we all worked. It was heart-breaking to do that. But it needed to be done.

My adoptive mum had fallen pregnant again in 2008. This pregnancy took us all by surprise, and we welcomed a baby boy in September. After my adoptive mum had given birth, I unfortunately didn't have that much time with the baby boy as I had with the baby girl. I made up for it where I could. They both loved me, and these two babies are now grown up. They call me Didi, which means sister. And you cannot tell them that I am not their sister. You are asking for trouble. I am their Didi and that is just how it is. They are my world, my light. They are my everything. I love these children so much, a part of me feels that they are my brother and sister that have been reincarnated. There is so much that I see in them that I saw in my siblings.

We went frequently to Johannesburg to visit family. The one day, we visited my eldest aunt and her husband told me that one of his friend's daughters had a baby. She was 16 years old. I said, "ok nice, good for her!" Then he says, "See, even that girl is beating you in having children."

Well, I was 21 years old. I had no intention of falling pregnant until I was married. If this child felt that she wanted to have a baby, or it happened as things do happen without a plan, it was her decision. I just felt that this eldest aunt and uncle from Johannesburg hated that I was so prosperous. It seemed they could not stand to see me rise and make something of myself one day. They always expected the worst for me.

Time went on and I enjoyed working and earning my own money. I worked hard. A few months into my new job, my adoptive dad received news on a job offer at another company. He resigned and needed to relocate, but I was not ready to move with them. After all,

I had just started a job in this petrochemical company. They trusted me to stay alone with my adoptive mum's cousin, as he had also started a job in the same company. We travelled to work together and kept each other company. This is where the rumour had surfaced from, that I had a man staying with me.

At one stage, our working times changed and my adoptive mum's cousin started earlier than I did. I had to find other means of getting to work.

I didn't have my license then. I spoke to my adoptive dad about how travelling to work was going to be an issue for me and, after speaking to a few friends he once worked with, my travelling was arranged. I was grateful that I had transport. Later on, that also went sour because the one guy started to like me. He was married to a very beautiful and nice lady, but he begged to differ. He said he never loved her! I was young and very stupid but not stupid enough to break a home. I should know better because an affair broke my home.

As time went by, he started to visit me during my lunch break in my office. One day, he closed my office door behind him. He professed his love for me. He grabbed me and started to kiss me.

Like I said, I was stupid!
I gave in and kissed him back.

Whenever we had to wait for the other guys that were part of our travel club, he would woo me and I loved it, but at the back of my mind, all I could picture was his wife and what she would feel like. One day, he tried to kiss me and I pushed him away.

I told him that he needed to focus on his wife and his marriage. I would not break a home. He was furious with me. I didn't care. I was an adult and wrong was wrong. I wouldn't want something like this to happen to me. This guy stopped travelling with us and the other guys wanted to know what happened, so, I told them. They agreed that what I did was wrong, knowing he was married and that he too should focus on his marriage. I am glad I stopped that relationship and stood up to a man that was doing wrong to his wife.

My adoptive parents moved back to Kinross. We were a family again. I groomed myself to become an independent woman. Later in 2008 after I turned 21, I booked for driving lessons, got my learners and went on to get my license. My first shot at getting my license failed.

You know that incline!
Remember to use your handbrake.
Anyway, I never gave up, I tried again and I passed.
I was a licensed driver. The little achievements made me proud and I felt good about myself.

Some things I looked back on:
- Living through my trauma and dealing with stuff I never thought I would face.
- Failing Grade 11, prompted me to step back in and do exceptionally well.
- Living from home to home, facing challenges.
- Falling in love and experiencing heartbreak taught me to be tough on my heart.
- Learning when to say no for the right reasons.

Everything I did was one step closer to where I wanted to be. Not only were all my life lessons an eye opener, I was also learning about who I am. I made it a point to set goals for every new year, and, as they were done, I ticked them off.

I was no longer that 13 year old girl that liked the color blue and loved dolphins just because everyone else did. I was now someone who could tell you, that I loved all colors but my favorite color was yellow. My favorite animal was not a dolphin. I didn't have a favorite because I was an animal lover, so I love them all. I discovered things about myself I never knew. While everyone was studying in University, I enrolled to do part-time studies.

I was working and I was earning my own money. This meant that I could buy whatever I wanted without anybody telling me no!
I bought clothes that I liked.
I bought shoes and jewelry.
I bought a ring to act like I was engaged so that the men could leave me alone. But that never happened. After that episode with a married man, I decided that enough was enough.

Some men just don't know the word no, and some women as well. If both genders entertain each other and don't respect that one or both, are in a committed relationship, then I don't know. I do know that it was wrong.

I loved working and pampering myself. The best part was that I was still the smart, savvy saver. I saved and I remembered what my mummy had told me, "There is a time for boys, just travel."

So, I did. I saved up, and my first destination was India. By March 2009, I had saved up around R70 000.

Ever since then, I made it a point that every year, or when I can afford it, I will travel. I have been to various International and national destinations.

Birthdays became important to me once again. My adoptive parents held a small party for me with all those that cared for me.

Life was different. It felt like the hardships had vanished. Had I gone through with my suicide attempts, I would have missed out on all of this.

In 2009, for my birthday, I purchased my first vehicle. I paid monthly installments and insurance for a car that I washed and pickled because I was too scared to drive! It scared me to death, driving next to trucks and crowded places. All that changed in December 2009, when I was forced to drive because of work times changing over the festive season. We could finish early every second day. At that time, I was working in a new department. I had moved from Maintenance Planning to I.T. My goal was to learn everything and every plant that this company had. My dream was to become a manager. Every time I walked past the management building, I imagined myself sitting in one of those "larnie" offices. In order for me to be a good manager, I had to understand and learn everything about this company, from the bottom. Every two years, I would apply for jobs within this company's umbrella, in order to learn something new. My knowledge grew and it also helped me to understand how each department functioned and its processes.

There was something that a colleague mentioned to me while working in our I.T. department:

"A birthday is your day, so celebrate your life. Put in a day's leave or whatever it is, and spoil yourself!"

I did just that. Every year since 2009, I got my mojo back for birthdays and I spoiled myself.

Some of my accomplishments didn't sit too well with some of my family. After all, I was not working to please anyone but myself. I owed myself that.

My life changed even more in 2009, when Schivan crossed my path once again! This time it was on a serious note and neither of us was willing to back down. We were no longer in school, not teens but adults.

At this point I was still dating that guy that was so set on us getting the proposal done and his mum had purchased my sari. Remember that?

Well, while I was dating that guy, Mr Schivan made contact with me again. Tough decisions had to be made: Do I continue to be with this person that can't visit me in hospital over his sore throat, or do I try again with the person my adoptive parents hate?

My adoptive parents seemed to like every boy I brought home, but I was never completely happy. There was always something I found out of place that didn't sit well with my expectations or should I rather say: nobody matched the filled that checklist that Schivan had aced.

Schivan was ready to try again. He was aware that I was in a relationship and put this offer on the table.

We started chatting and basically picking up where we had left off. He asked me if I still felt the same about him, after all these years. I had mentioned to him that I was in a relationship, there could be a possibility that I might marry this guy I was currently dating, and he insisted that I bring my boyfriend to his 21st birthday party in Standerton, just so he could see me one more time!

I told my adoptive parents that Schivan had invited me to his 21st, and asked if I could go. The answer was no. I left it as that. I was 21 years old at that time, so I understood that I couldn't just go. I lived under my adoptive parents' roof, and I had to respect that, even though my boyfriend at that time was willing to take me to the party.

Schivan's birthday was in February, so we kept on chatting. All that time I still dated the other guy, though I eventually broke off the relationship with him. There was a very close female friend that he was fond of and supported. She always took priority over me. To be honest, it couldn't have come at a better time, and I told him we should just part ways because I still loved Schivan. That deep down, I could feel it.

Honestly every guy I dated, I compared to Schivan. Nobody came close to him. I decided that we should meet up. This time it had to be a fool-proof plan and we could not get caught. A friend helped me to come up with a plan. I felt so bad for lying to my adoptive parents, but I just had to. I had to see if I felt the same after all these years. Speaking to someone over the phone and having them in front of you are completely different experiences. We were 21, not 17, if it was meant to be, it would!

My adoptive parents were going to Johannesburg to visit family. I didn't want to go, because my best friend was coming over to stay. This friend I hold close to my heart because he stood by me. This was the same friend's house I would jump off at, after school. My adoptive parents knew him well, so they were fine with us staying at home, but what they didn't know was that Schivan was coming home to meet me. I hated lying, and the thought of being caught again sent my heart into a frenzy, but it seemed like a fool-proof plan. My adoptive parents left for Johannesburg, and after some time, Schivan pulled in. I was so nervous. The last time I had told Schivan to come over, it was a disaster. My friend went to visit his cousin, which allowed Schivan and I to have some time together.

We spoke and cuddled for the first time, we even kissed for the first time. In all those years, since 2004, it was only then, that I got to have an actual real kiss from Camera Boy! It was our first real kiss, and everything felt right. It felt perfect, like a puzzle that comes together. We couldn't keep our hands off each other. Before he left, he told me to let him know if I wanted to date again. He told me he still loved me very much. He gave me time to think and I agreed that we would date again, but this time we would tell our parents and we would not hide. We officially started dating and I told my adoptive parents that we wanted to date each other. He told his parents. His parents seemed fine, but my adoptive parents had an issue. They requested that he bring his parents home to make everything legal so that we could date. Schivan and I were against that because to us, making everything legal felt like we were being forced to get married, and we only wanted to date at that stage. We only wanted to see if this was what we both wanted, where it could go. If we were still together years later, then there could be a wedding.

This upset Schivan's parents and mine. Schivan decided to come home and ask my adoptive parents for permission to date me. My adoptive parents approved, but still requested that his parents come home. It blew things out of proportion.

I spoke to my adoptive parents and told them that we were not serious about marriage at that stage. We just wanted to date. That was all. When we felt we were ready for his parents to come home, we would arrange it. In the end, it was fine, and we started dating, but we were not allowed to be alone, go to the movies or supper. We had to either be at home or one of the children had to be with us. This went on for months. It started to frustrate me and Schivan.

I was 22 years old when I had lost my virginity to Schivan. He was my first. And I am not ashamed to say that I had kept my virginity for so long. I was proud that I kept it, to share it with the person I loved, a person I felt I had a connection with. I know that in this day and age, sex is just a pleasure game. Saving yourself for someone special, has meaning.

Schivan and I would have arguments, he would also say nasty things and it hurt my feelings. He would make it feel like I was at fault for things. He never took the blame for anything, but again, I was stupid and silly and blinded in love because I always apologized and said it was my fault. He called me an emotional wreck once!

I always ran back. I let it be, because I loved him. One day in our office we were chatting about my issues and one of my colleagues said, "Why don't you move out?" That way you are living your life, with your rules and your relationship with your adoptive parents will improve. Eventually, I made up my mind to move out of my adoptive parents' home and move into a flat. It was such a bold move, it scared the shit out of me. Apart from buying a car that I seldom drove, this was one of the scariest things I had done.

I needed to become independent. I needed to do this for me and for my relationship. Maybe I was selfish, because in the process I hurt so many people choosing Schivan and my independence, including hurting my precious little siblings that loved me so dearly. My heart was in so many pieces.

Call this what you may, but I do believe that if you let it go and it comes back to you, it's yours to keep. I prayed and asked for guidance. Everyone in my family, including Ma, got wind that I was moving out of my adoptive parents' home.

My eldest aunt got involved. She would call Schivan and I. She would say I was bringing down the family name, and that I was such a disgrace.

Things just blew out of proportion. I reminded myself that I needed to be independent, I needed to see if the person I claimed to love, was indeed who I truly loved, that the family around me would either support or leave me. I had Swami with me, to guide and protect me.

The idea had started a whole new chapter in my independence. Was moving out of a home that had sheltered me for years a good move? Would my relationship work? If I didn't try I would never know. It was the first time I had made a decision for myself. It was the first time I came first. I mattered.

There are times when we all fail to realize that we must come first. All my life, I had put everyone else's feelings first, but that day, I made a decision and I stuck to it. My eldest aunt had called once again to shout at me. My Ma called to say that if I moved out, she would wash her hands of me and that I was "doing this because of a boy who didn't come from a good family!"

Had anyone taken the time to get to know Schivan, instead of just hearing what others said?
What did I choose?
Family or Love?

This pushed me more to the edge. Once again, I felt like dying because I was being pulled between family and what I wanted. I didn't know whether I should listen to family or follow my heart.

I chose to follow my heart.

Schivan fetched me from home one day and took me to by some essentials. My adoptive parents were not too happy that Schivan actually supported me moving out. It was a huge decision. In our family, we were brought up in such a way that girls only moved out of their parents' home when they got married.

That notion needs to stop. For how long will we hold back our girls from becoming independent?

Do women still need to be dependent on a man? No! Times are changing. We cannot live the way our great grandparents and grandparents lived. Teach your girls that it is okay to venture out, but don't slander your name and rub it in the mud while enjoying your independence. I promised myself that! Even though I was moving out in the name of love, my reputation and the way I carried myself for a young lady living on her own would not be brought down. Instead, people were to see me and be proud that I was living alone and I still carried my morals and values.

I would not rub the Sewdass name in the mud. I would make my late parents proud while being independent.

A friend I had schooled with, started working with me and she needed to move as well, so we decided to move in together and split the rent. We split the groceries as well. It was in June 2010 when I moved out, and it was sad for me because everyone I loved was unhappy with my decision. My little brother and sister cried because their Didi was leaving. I was unsure if I was allowed to see them again. Those children were my life. I moved out and my adoptive parents assisted me with the move but refused to step into my new home. They dropped of my household goods and left. The children cried; they couldn't understand why I had left. I had made a huge impact in their lives.

Months went by, and I travelled to see the children in Kinross, as I couldn't live without them. I did this a few times, until one day my adoptive parents told me that I could no longer see the children. It became too upsetting and it had been affecting them. They thought it best I stay away. And since I had chosen a boy that had a terrible family due to their "violence", they couldn't have their children in harm's way.

I understood and respected their wishes. I was wrong to move out of a home that sheltered me all those years when nobody wanted me. I was wrong to choose love. I burnt my fingers and dug my grave. If this relationship failed, I would have no place to hide my embarrassed face.

My life shattered again. I was finally happy with the man I always wanted to be with, but now my family could not see my happiness.

Once again, I wanted to die.

I drank every weekend and week day to drown my sorrows, though I still woke up, prayed and went to work. There were days I cried in my open plan office. It became so bad. I felt suffocated and started having terrible anxiety attacks. I would drive to Kinross, and drive past their home, hoping to see the children playing outside. If I saw them, that was enough. I would go to their friend's house in Kinross town, and the girls and I would go do our hair, I'd stay over and we would drink responsibly while under the watchful eye of their parents. To Stich and family, thank you for always being there. I know if it wasn't for you and your family, I would have been dead.

The sort of exile was so hard for me. I loved those 2 children so much. Day in day out I prayed that they would make peace with me. One weekend, I was alone in the flat, and I heard a child call out Didi. I thought I was hearing things, then I heard it again, and again. I ran to the door, only to find my two angels standing at the door with tears in their eyes. How I cried! My heart longed for my brother and sister and they longed for their Didi. I cried as I took them in my arms (I have tears in my eyes reliving this moment. Even though it was years ago, I still feel this pain while writing). So much heartache was caused because I decided to do what I wanted. We made peace and I was once again allowed to see the children. More time went by and my friend got engaged, so I decided to move into a company flat.

There was a lot I needed to buy on my own, to furnish my new flat. I didn't have a fridge, washing machine, TV, Microwave, lounge set and a few other small things.

Living on my own made me realize and see the bigger picture of the world. There were times I was broke as hell. Living alone definitely had its pros and cons.

As a responsible adult, it was priority to make sure that my rent, car instalments and insurance were paid, I had a full tank of petrol, prepaid electricity topped up and groceries for the month. Since I had to buy things to furnish my flat at first, cash was very tight. Luxuries were the last on my list. Schivan's dad gave me a bar stool, so I at least had something to sit on. What I urgently needed was a fridge, and soon after I got that, I bought a washing machine. Everything else just followed. I couldn't purchase everything in one swipe. A friend was kind enough to donate her grandmother's antique lounge set to me. Finally, after months of struggling, I had something to relax on. My flat started to look like a home.

With my left-over salary, I would budget for the other things I needed to do for the month. Some months I was left with only R100 in my account. It was not because I had over spent, neither was it due to unpaid accounts. I never created accounts. My father once told me "If you can't afford it, stay without it." I lived by that.

Something that most people don't know is that I secretly helped out in the community. Every month I would try to at least buy someone a meal, a loaf of bread and milk, a blanket during winter or socks. I never did it to post my good deeds. I did it because I felt I was well off to have food on my table and I could share the little I had with someone who had nothing. When I donated whatever it was, I never judged their appearance.

There were some months that I didn't have petrol money. I never borrowed money from anyone because I never knew if I could pay it back.

My parents always kept money and rice grains at our prayer place. Even if it was a R10 my dad would place it at our lamp. Swami provided us with a job and food to sustain us, keeping a coin or note and rice was a way to say thank you and may our money and food never run out. I carried this practice into my own home. The days when I needed money to fill up my car, I would borrow the money from this sacred spot. I would pray and ask for forgiveness, more so not to be punished because it is a sin to use this money for anything unless its prayer related. I felt so bad in my heart to do this on certain months and prayed that I would never be punished for using this money for something else. I always put that prayer money back into the account of Swami. As soon as I received my salary, I would put in the money I took and add a little extra.

I was glad to have friends who were understanding. We all had financial issues. During the months that we couldn't make our month-end supper, it was ok, we covered for each other or just moved it to the next month. We always celebrated our monthly good news and, of course, our birthdays.

Do you know, I never knew how to do a bank deposit? My adoptive dad always did it for me. When I moved out of my adoptive parents' home, I had to learn how to do it! I had to do grocery shopping. I had to cook, which was something I never did in my adoptive parents' home.

Moving out did me good. Learning to become independent did me good. I grew up and matured. There were times when I came home, drunk as a skunk from a party or work function. I never got to experience that in my teen years, like everyone else. When I moved out for love, it was also a move for me to experience things. Most importantly, I found myself. All my life I had searched for love, approval and looked for acceptance from everyone. But the reality was that, in order for me to be at peace, I needed to accept me for me. Nobody's approval actually mattered. What mattered was loving myself.

During my independent lifestyle I tried out so many things.

I smoked weed for the first time.
I partied for the first time.
I drank until I got sick.
I went out and did what I did not do, at the same time I still kept my head held high and did not bring my father's name down.

In my family's eyes, I made my mother roll in her grave with my independence. Some experiences I would never want to repeat. They were not for me and I would never make them a habit. However, I did discover my love of wine.

Moving out made me stronger but also lonely, due to the lack of support. I travelled again, this time with my friend. We went on our first ship cruise. Her sister and brother-in-law joined us for that trip and it was amazing in Mozambique. The rocking of the ship makes you sick, but we stayed drunk and partied till sunrise.

I never gave up on Prayer. Every morning I would say the following: "Swami, please look after my brother and sister, Please let them know that I love and I miss them a lot. Please always guide them and protect them from any harm. One day they will accept Schivan and see him as I do!"

Their parents may have stopped me from seeing them, but it never stopped me from praying for them. My independence definitely played an important part towards creating the woman I am today.

Through every hardship faced, I always thought about and questioned my late parents. Part of me at that time still hated the fact that they just left me! There were nights I yelled out to the heavens in a howling cry because of the pain that I still felt. The thought of a quick overdose or hanging myself from the railing of my loft often crossed my mind.

I was angry at them. I was angry at my parents, and I carried this anger. I couldn't make peace. Their deaths truly affected me, every day and every step I took in my life. The longing for them to be here with me. I don't know if I would have taken this "moving out" move if my parents were alive, but living under the roof of my adoptive parents, and the constant fighting, needed to stop. I had to make that sacrifice to save that relationship.

I missed my mums' comfort for all the heartache I experienced.
She was not there. My father was not there to tell Schivan, that this was his daughter, that he must not hurt me. My mother wasn't there to have those girly chats or to give sex advice. Do you know who I had to ask? I asked my female work colleagues for sex advice and tips.

I wish my father could have been there, to air it on a speaker of how proud he was of his daughter, and that the man that marries her will be getting a gem of a wife.

I was extremely grateful that my dad left me with the knowledge of cars, though. Whenever something was wrong with my car, I was able to identify that something didn't sound right.

Who could fulfill the roles of parents in my life for basic life skills?

Something else I had to learn, later on, was that you need to be neat down there! How was I supposed to know that?

There were talks I wish my mother was around to give me, because the mothers that did take care of me, never told me a lot. I used Google and the art of listening to chit chat in the office. My fatherly figure was not there to stand guard and tell me that if things didn't work out, that I could come back home.

I let my relationship with my adoptive parents be.

My independence opened 10 million other wounds. Why did my real parents leave me to suffer such extreme pain? Weren't their deaths enough? I cried almost every night when I had moved out and the suicidal thoughts came gushing in. I got so frustrated the one night that I took a photo of my mother and ripped it up, and threw it into the bin. If I had gone through with my suicide attempt, I completely believed that nobody would have taken note. It would have alerted my work colleagues and my boyfriend Schivan. Nobody else. As far as family went, ties were cut and I let it be.

Becoming independent wasn't a bad choice, I decided that if my relationship didn't work out with Schivan, I had saved enough to move overseas and start afresh.

Always have a backup plan for the failed plans, save money for a rainy day, never give up on love and prayer, show up even if you are fighting a war, come out stronger than before.

The more people put me down, or thought I would fail, the more I pushed myself to be successful.

There are things I still carry with me from the people and different homes I was raised in, but everything else I owe to the independence I gave myself. I taught myself lessons and grew balls I never knew I had. I say this because I never knew how to say NO and I would do whatever was needed to keep my family relationships peaceful and happy, even if it made me sad. Eventually, I had cut ties that were so painful it almost killed me. I had to learn to live without family again. Yes, I caused the pain for myself that time, but was it right for my family to treat me the way they did?

I know they never saw things from my perspective. It was so much easier to understand the adults' points of view and listen to the nonsense that was spewed about their disrespectful so-called daughter. I know that it was easy to be proud of me, only when I listened, and did as I was told. But when I chose my own happiness over everyone else's, they had no problem throwing me to the curb. The way I saw it, only those who have never sinned, have the right to judge me. I have sinned, so I don't judge others, and I know that my family have sinned too. Only my creator, my God, will pass judgement on me.

My silence grew louder when I was alone. I am glad I was able to turn down the volume and choose to continue, despite everything thrown at me. Living alone was a huge, huge, huge eye opener for me, not only mentally, but emotionally too. Some of my worst times came from being alone with myself, the person that everyone disliked.

I never meant for my independence and choosing to fight for love to hurt anybody. It was just time for me to prioritize ME!

REFLECTION

For every problem faced, suicide should not be the answer! In any home it should be normalized that it is okay for girls and boys to become independent. We are stereotyped from such a young age. It's okay for girls to play with cars and boys to play with dolls, it's okay for girls to like blue and boys' pink. At the end of the day, we all need to learn to take care of ourselves, cooking, household chores, grocery shopping etc.

PART 2

13

NEW BEGINNINGS

Schivan proposed on 14 February 2013. We were on a cruise. It was a two-week cruise, and we visited Madagascar, Le Reunion and Mauritius. This was such an amazing cruise. The food… oh my goodness! We tasted the best lobster ever, in Madagascar. I will definitely go there again for the lobster. Ironically, I had almost given up on my relationship at this point because it didn't seem like he wanted to commit. We had such a huge fight just before we left South Africa, and I knew that, once the cruise was done, we would probably go our separate ways. What I didn't know was that he had planned to propose and made me lose all hope on purpose, to make the surprise spectacular. I made the best of my holiday. On Valentine's day according to him, while we were on tour for the submarine, that's where he wanted to propose, but because of the rush, he had forgotten the ring. So, the second try was at the Valentine's day dinner. I said yes, obviously, and I wondered how he had managed to hide the ring, because I am so observant. Clever him! He hid the ring in his vanity case and he had kept it on the highest shelf. I didn't think of looking there and anyway, I am too short to even reach that high.

Everyone was excited that we were going to get married. Some I think, not so happy because those people didn't expect that I would actually get married. Those same people didn't believe in the relationship and didn't think it would go any further.

In the very same year, during the month of September, my Nana (Maternal Grandfather) passed away. His death didn't affect me as much as I thought it would. It did hurt, but not as much as it did when I lost my family. When my Nana got sick, I prepared myself for the worst. If he were to die, I was ready to receive the news. My Nana was old after all, and I had made peace that, at his age it was only time that kept him here.

On the day of his funeral, everyone stood together. It felt like the family I once knew. I guess I had messed up that moment as well when I decided not to spend the mourning days with my Ma, all my Mosi's and Mama. Schivan was there as my support and I decided to leave with him to Rustenburg instead of staying in Johannesburg. They didn't need me there and I was already the black sheep, the last thing everyone needed was an argument to break out about me dating Schivan. So, I left the scene. Days later, when I checked in with my adoptive mum; to find out how my Ma was doing, I got an earful.

"If you cared about Ma you should have stayed. Don't ask about her if you don't care." Yes, I should have stayed, but I felt that it was not my place. It was a time for them to mourn their father. I took my mourning to Rustenburg where I could cry without being given dagger looks or hollow comments. I let it be.

Weeks and months went by and I called Ma to check on her. It's not easy to lose a spouse and especially at that age, after years of being together.

As per tradition we had to have a proposal for me and Schivan. The boy's side of the family must come to the girl's family to formally confirm that we wish to marry and confirm the wedding date. Since the passing of my Nana, we were not allowed to have any celebrations until the one-year mourning period was over. However, the priest advised that it was ok to have our proposal after the 6-month ceremony, on condition that it was fine with my Ma. Ma gave us her blessings to continue. We decided that, because I had lived with my adoptive parents, we would have the proposal there, but Schivan had an issue with that idea because when I moved out my adoptive father said that Schivan should never set foot in their house. So Schivan felt that he could not set foot in a place he was not welcome, and he could definitely not bring his entire family. He felt that we did not have their blessing, and so the arguments started again. My adoptive parents did not approve of our relationship. They had refused to support me in this and told me I should ask my Ma, as she was my legal guardian. So, this is how it worked. I was adopted, meaning I had adoptive parents and they had a say over most things, but when it came to this, "my legal guardian" had to take over. Simple Simon.

Upon hearing this, I spoke to Ma and she was extremely disheartened by this because they had adopted me. Why were they being so difficult? It was their home, something I didn't have a right over since I moved out. Ma and her brothers stepped in to assist. Ma's brothers were upset that I was not given any support in my relationship or towards my proposal and wedding. Arrangements went on for the proposal and Ma requested that her son be present. I refused to have him there. My reason for that was he was never around me growing up. Why now, should he stand there as an elder for me? At this point in my life, if you didn't play a role in my formative life, I didn't need you to be a part of my new one. I was done with putting on a show.

I know that Ma meant well, because she was a widow, she was unable to do certain things which though this is something I disagree with. Ma had and has, every right to stand as my elder regardless of her being a widow. Some traditions need to stop! My Ma was a widow but she was still a mother, she was my motherly figure and because she was a widow it was disregarded for her to perform certain rituals, especially that of giving her daughter away to her future husband on their wedding day.

I offered to pay for the décor and everything that Ma was planning for the proposal. Ma refused and said she would do it for her child, and she did. Many family members, especially her children, thought I was using Ma just to get everything done. I was not. I recall at some point being torn again between family and my love. Ma and I did have arguments. One minute it was like this, then that, then I had to listen to Schivan and his family's requests, then run it by my family. Oh Gosh! Just before the event, my adoptive parents decided they did in fact, want to be a part of it. I was happy, but also sad because they couldn't accept my husband to-be. I felt there was no need to show their faces if they were just coming to show face. I told them to not attend it. Word was, if they attended my father-in-law would hit them or they would be removed and put in the ICU. You know, in a family feud words are always said. Yes, Schivan did mention that if my adoptive parents pitched up he would put them in the ICU. I was also scared that he would harm my family. The argument between myself, Schivan and my adoptive parents was if this boy could say such things, then he had no respect for my adoptive parents and no respect for me. How could I marry a person like this, that was so violent? Pulled in all three directions, I turned to drinking again to numb myself. I just couldn't end my relationship with Schivan. I loved him. I couldn't see my family hurt because I loved them too. I didn't want to see them in the ICU, I mean if it wasn't for them, I wouldn't have had a home to live in. Could everyone not put aside their issues and look at me? I was willing to walk out on everyone, including my family and Schivan.

There were even family members that added things that were not even said. I didn't know who to trust, who to believe about what rumors went on! Once again, I was in this dilemma, at a breaking point of almost calling everything quits.

One night I had just about had enough. I gave him the ring and all his belongings and sent him home to Standerton. I did this because he lied to me. There was this girl that was working with him. She was a very beautiful Indian girl, and call me jealous but I sensed something more was going on from this girl. Every night we spoke all I ever heard was this girl's name and he would go on and on about her. He said they were just friends and I had nothing to worry about, that she had a boyfriend and she knew he had a fiancé. They travelled together and whenever he came through to Johannesburg, he would give her a lift home as it was on his way to Standerton. So I let it be. He was in Rustenburg and I was in Secunda, so I had to trust him and he trusted me in our long-distance relationship. Time went on, and I found that I couldn't get hold of him because he was so often on the phone with this girl, or he would pitch up with blue pinch marks on his hands because she had pinched him while he was driving. These things started to get on my nerves in a big way, because I had a 3-strike rule. If I had to warn him about something 3 times, then I was done. So anyway, this friendship went on even after he told me that he was no longer friends with her and he deleted her number and so on.

One morning at work I saw a strange email from a guy. He was not on my contact list and neither was he a supplier. I opened the mail and to find out that my dear fiancé was still speaking to her, and this mail was from her boyfriend. He had sent me the SMS's between them. That was proof enough. On top of all the chatting, he ended his conversations with "hugs" and "mwah" (kisses).

All hell broke loose in my mind. I let him have it. All he could say was that they were just friends and that he only kept in touch with her because she had nice Chutney music (Indian folk music). The cold fact was that he had lied to me, after I had told him to end this friendship with her because I sensed there was something more. I told him to decide what and who he wanted because I was done! That night when he came to see me, I sent him off with his things. His words to me were, "Remember, you wanted this!"

As he drove off, I cried. His dad called to ask what had happened and I explained the story. His dad said they were just friends, that he had told him that as well. Yes, I understood they were friends, but I could not accept a friendship where she called him in the middle of the night for help with this and that, and he was prone to dropping her off. His dad said he would speak to Schivan when he got home. I had nobody around me. It was a miserable night alone. Schivan is a cold-hearted person when it comes to certain things. He can walk away and not look back. During our dating days, he broke up with me numerous times. He called me an emotional wreck during our wedding planning, and even before that, but I was a sucker for holding onto him. Deep down I wanted this to work. I wanted this relationship so badly it felt like only he fitted the best in my soul. The weekend went by and we sorted things out. He wasn't able to utter the words *I am sorry*. I loved him, but at the same time I knew his temper. I also couldn't deal with my family and their issues with me. It felt like whatever and however my marriage worked out, I just needed to get married and see from there. What was worse? Schivan's temper or being the constant black sheep of my family?

The day of the engagement arrived. My eldest aunt helped to dress me up. All my close family was around me and my Ma. That was all I needed. The formalities were done and dusted. Ma was sad that day. I remember her looking at me and admiring me.
"If only your parents could see you."

Ma and I had our occasional arguments again when we didn't agree on something or when I was under pressure from Schivan about the wedding plans.

Our wedding date was set for December 13th, 2014. Again, I tried to invite my adoptive parents, but they didn't want in on anything for my wedding because they heard that they were not welcome and would be escorted out. Yes, they did annoy people with their ways, but nobody would stop them from attending their child's wedding. If they really and truly wanted to, they would have. Once again, I was not allowed to see the children because of the children's safety. The attached email from my adoptive father, shows that they were hurt by all of this and I allowed my relationship with Schivan to go ahead despite all that had been said to them.

Sewdass, Alicia (A)

From:
Sent: 23 June 2014 11:09 AM
To: Sewdass, Alicia (A)
Cc:

Subject: the good life

Alicia
Talking to you all these years has not brought any relief so far so I think it's best that i put this in writing
Please take this as a serious issue as we are trying to keep out of all your problems
I do not want my children to visit you from now on , we prefer that all of us keep our distances from each other as outsiders are threatening us with violence, bloodshed ,ICU we do not know what more can take place
If we as parents of ████ ████ can be sworn at , threatened , accused and abused by outsiders then my children also need to be protected from this
I do not think that you have taken these threats seriously but we as parents have taken it quite seriously and do not want any interference from these type of people
We do not tell you what to do in life so please do not question our way of life , it is our business
In future whatever goes on in your life please do not bring us into it as we listen and hear the threats against us and if you do not oppose it , I take it that you support it
You know all that has been said against us but you hide behind the truth and have absolutely no feelings for what we go through and still demand that we bow down to you and these outsiders
Please do not take advantage of our good natures anymore and start living your life without us as your family
It is also time for you to take your postal address elsewhere so that we do not have any issues anymore
What-ever belongs to you in our home , please pick it up ASAP
Sorry for being so blunt but we are really stressed out and need to let you know how we feel!
My decisions are final and I do not want any more said on this mail , i will not reply it or make an issue of this again
Hope that you have a good life ahead

Every time I felt the need to go home, I would read this and stop myself from visiting. I understand that they were hurt and with whatever being said by my then soon-to-be in-laws, I did not support it. But like I've said before, you can't be all in one minute and then out the next then you want in again. I was stressed, my adoptive parents were stressed and I was not willing to give up my love for family. I had to choose family or love. I may have been wrong for not siding with my family but would I have been married today to the one I love, or not?

I felt more sure about Schivan than any of the other guys I had dated. I felt that in my heart, and I felt I had to continue this relationship with him. I cried and prayed. Only the pillows and Swami know how I pulled through every day of my life. Pushing, just trying to go on. Every day I prayed that my adoptive parents would see through all the rumors, see that Schivan was a good person and so was his family.

It saddened me that I had to get the things done on my own. My Ma bless her soul, had offered to have all my pre-wedding ceremonies from her home. She was going to do everything she could to make my day special. I had her support, and Ma's brothers supported us as well. They had also played such a vital role in the preparation of this wedding. If it wasn't for these people, I would have fallen apart. The year of my marriage made me hit rock bottom. I suffered a lot from anxiety and depression. Schivan was sometimes not too supportive and added more fuel to my emotional state. I felt like the walls locked me into a tight spot, I was cornered and had nowhere to go. I preferred to sleep. I contemplated hanging myself again, I lived in a loft so it was easy.

I prayed. All my life I prayed for strength and it carried me through. All that I have today is from prayer. Swami just said *keep going* and I would sleep, wake up and go on. Schivan and I had our quarrels, normal wedding issues on how things should be done. He didn't realize how much effort I was putting in. He had nothing to worry about because he had his parents to sort everything for him. They knew their role. Schivan basically just needed to show up on the day. I on the other hand, had to do everything. He never understood why I was under pressure. He never saw the depressed, anxiety stricken and suicidal me. Even telling him this, I would be asked why I was so weak.

I allowed him to break me some more. He couldn't understand why I still wanted my adoptive parents at my wedding. All he could see was that they didn't accept him, so they shouldn't be there. I saw the man I loved and my heartbroken adoptive parents, but because I heard words of harm being mentioned against them, I knew they should not be involved, even if just for their own safety.

My heart broke each day and I prayed that there might be some light between the two families and that there could be peace.

I longed to see my brother and sister as I wanted them to be part of the wedding, but my adoptive parents refused. My heart cried. I did everything with a heavy heart. My adoptive parents bought me a wedding sari the year before. They decided to get it sewn and then I would wear that. At that point, I thought it was a good deed of them despite all that was going on. My adoptive mum and eldest aunt went to India and the sari went in for sewing. They had returned to Johannesburg with no Sari as it was still to be sewn and shipped. My eldest aunt was responsible for getting it to South Africa. As time drew closer to the wedding, it was just story upon story from her. Eventually I told her to keep the Sari, that I would buy my own.

Schivan's parents took us shopping and his parents bought my wedding clothes. I heard nothing about the Sari. I too was at a point, and I was not going to give in to my adoptive parents' requests. My wedding would go on!

I had mixed emotions about it because on one hand, they don't support and accept my relationship, and on the other hand they wanted to be part of it. People took their own views about this, but how do you accept something that isn't given to you wholeheartedly? I knew they loved me and they wanted to give me the best, but how could I accept it when my relationship itself was not accepted? It was already enough that the man I chose to marry was not accepted. If they wished me well, they had a funny way of showing it. One minute it was all good and happy and the next moment they didn't want to accept it. If it didn't go their way, it was not going to happen but this was my day, not theirs. I understood this off-and-on thing irritated my soon to-be husband and his family. Eventually Schivan told me that they either supported me fully or not at all, because it was tearing me apart.

That made sense to me, so when Schivan's parents took me shopping to buy my outfit, I got to pick my outfit and the color, and that is when I truly felt like a bride. Schivan had purchased his traditional attire as well, so that we matched perfectly.

I kept everything updated on an excel spreadsheet. Everything that I had to pay for or arrange, was managed on that sheet. Since I was not in my adoptive parents' good books, Ma said that my wedding would take place from her home. She would sort everything out for my pre-marital ceremonies and the wedding hall. I felt the wedding hall was too much for Ma to handle, so I took that away and added it to my and Schivan's costs. A lot of things were split as a couple.

What I admired the most was the unity and support he had from all his family. I only had my Ma and her brothers. None of my aunts jumped in for preparations or costs. I understood the financial issues and I was not the niece that everyone liked because I spoke my mind and more so, because the issues with my adoptive parents affected everyone's decisions to attend my wedding. So I was prepared for no support from anyone. I worked hard and late hours to bring in extra money for my wedding and to help Ma. Ma's brothers and I had countless meetings to see where we were with the planning. Not once did my aunts add anything, and my adoptive parents were excluded completely. On one meeting, I remember us finalizing everything and Ma's brother shouted at my aunts for not supporting and guiding me. I needed someone to stand as my parents on the wedding day. It is customary for the bride's parents to hand her over to her new husband. Everyone was quiet. There was not even an offer to buy paper plates. That is how it was. Ma's brother told my eldest aunt that they should support and guide me in this, that I couldn't be planning everything on my own and they should stand as my parents. If they were not going to agree, I had asked my Ma's brother and his wife to stand for me.

My Ma had a heart attack just around October and I needed to send out my wedding invitations. We needed to ask my eldest aunt to give those out too. This task is usually performed by the bride's parents or an elder, and it is normally their honor to give the invitations out personally, to everyone that is invited. Nobody volunteered.

To my Ma's sister-in- law and her family I will forever be grateful to you all.

They helped to print out my wedding cards and deliver them to the families we needed to invite. They took me to Durban to invite our Durban families. My Ma's brothers, sisters-in-law and their children helped me a lot because my own house people couldn't. Schivan and I did the remainder of Johannesburg and Kinross. I had asked my eldest aunt to do the people who were close by in her area. Schivan and I had gone personally to invite my adoptive parents for the wedding. They said they would not attend because they were not welcome at my wedding. I let it be. We had invited my adoptive dad's family as well. His youngest sister had also made it clear that, because my adoptive parents were not welcome to my wedding, they would also not attend.

I was going to get this aunt, my adoptive dad's youngest sister, to do my hair, make-up and make the traditional wedding garlands for the wedding. I didn't want it for free. I was going to pay for everything. I am not the kind of person to ask for free things. If I know it's your business, I expect you to charge me the full amount, regardless of me being friend or family. When she had mentioned she would not attend my wedding but was still willing to do my bridal hair and make-up, I told myself I would find someone else.

Time went on and Schivan took me to invite my dad's side of the family. You haven't heard about them because I had lost contact with them. I had found one of my cousins on social media and had kept in touch, but never visited. I really wanted my dad's family to be there for my wedding. I could not leave them out, but it was based on their own decision to attend. The last time I had seen them was at my family's funeral. We got to talking, and I asked my Kaki (My dad's eldest brother's wife), why they hadn't kept in touch or visited me after my parents' death.

My Kaki told me that they were requested by my eldest aunt to stay away. Being told this, they did as they were told and, to prevent any problems they respected what was said. For all those years, I was told that my father's family didn't care about me. Now I knew why. To date, I still visit them. I have adorable nieces and nephews.

At the end of September 2014, I resigned from the petrochemical company I had worked for, for an amazing 8 years. I had worked there since 2006. After resigning, I moved to Rustenburg. All the wedding planning on Schivan's side was a breeze. We bought the souvenirs and little sweet boxes and his cousins, aunts and uncles were hands-on in helping. Since I was unemployed, I was able to do a lot as well. Again, I wished my parents were around. I wished I had my biological parents with me for every step of my planning. My planning would have been a breeze if my parents and siblings were around and if my adoptive parents had been involved.

At that time, I wanted to kill myself because of the lack of support and interest. I was to blame for all this unhappiness and family tension. I was wrong to get married to Schivan. After Ma's heart attack, my eldest aunt was concerned that my Ma wouldn't be able to have my wedding from her home as planned and advised me to look elsewhere to host my pre-wedding ceremonies. She gave me an option, but on condition.

She said, "I will loan you my house on condition you pay for everything." In some cultures, you would see this as acceptable, but not in mine. I told her I could buy everything to serve the people for that night, but for everything else I didn't have extra money.

Her response to me was, "You just resigned, you have a lot of money so you can use your pension money." I was still waiting for my pension money. What the hell? Schivan was sitting with me during this conversation and all I saw was utter disgust on his face. He called his uncle in Ermelo and told him what was going on. His uncle was prepared to send me off from his home, no conditions no loans, no money. I sat and cried at our doorstep and called my Ma's brothers to ask them to intervene.

Ma was recovering well and heard what had happened. Ma refused point blank. She said she would get her grand-daughter married from her home. I was the first grandchild to get married and my Ma wanted me to leave from her home. All the drama for my wedding caused terrible anxiety attacks for me. I hadn't booked for my bridal nails, makeup for all three days and I needed to book for the ladies that wanted to do their hair. My cousins were not at all supportive in helping me find people in Johannesburg. Every time I had asked for the lady's number, there was some or other story. My eldest aunt's daughter was left in charge to get appointments for the hairdressers. It was never done. There was let down after let down.

A friend I had schooled with, told me she knew someone who did makeup, hair and also dressed brides. So Nini introduced me to her friend. Upon the introduction we realized we actually knew each other from my childhood. We did my hair and makeup trials. I was so

201

happy with her work. This came as another blessing from the Heavens. Nini carried my cost for all my hair and makeup for all three days. A little about Nini, I knew her since my high school days in Lenasia. She was and still is bubbly and full of smiles. She always had long beautiful nails and I admired them when she had them painted navy blue. She had amazing, long hair and was always so full of fun. She was one of the girls that had my back. Our nickname for her was "Nini". I attended her 16th birthday party. At that time, I was staying with Ma and Ma allowed me to go with my friend Tazz. Tazz was my best friend and I spent weekends with her and Ma knew her, so we were all good to go out. Tazz and I were inseparable at school.

Everything was falling apart with the planning of this wedding, but I saw miracles and blessings in disguise from my Earth Angels. I am forever indebted to you two. Nini did my nails, free of charge. At that time, she had a nail salon. I hope someday I can repay this huge blessing.

I write this with tears in my eyes because I didn't ask for this. These were friends I schooled with, friends that I had opened up to on my bad days because I couldn't cry at home. These friends never judged me, they are my Angels.

My friends are my guardian Angels. My friends hold a special place in my heart.

It was time to put the final touches to everything. We were down to a week. We had to go home to begin preparations. With our Hindu weddings, it's a big affair. Families start arriving from two weeks before to help prepare. Schivan dropped me off in Johannesburg and he went off to Standerton. Things that were not done had to be completed in the week of the wedding. Thank God I was there a week early. I had taken extra cash because I knew that things like this would happen. Anyway, everyone eventually pulled their weight. I knew my middle aunt couldn't help financially but she and her amazing in-laws made up by wrapping all my wedding gifts and making everything look amazing. I treasured their input. I felt loved, having all my family around me, and hoped that my adoptive parents would come through. No matter what, I had that hope flame burning on the inside of me.

My Mendhi night (decorate the bride's hands and feet with henna), was on Thursday 11 December. It was my parents' death day and everyone was emotional. Nevertheless, we celebrated. My dad's family came to my celebrations as well. My Ma's house was decorated with beautiful lights and everyone was happy and laughing. It's so ironic, the 11 December 1999, I had lost my family to the murder-suicide and my pre-wedding ceremonies started on this very day. If this wasn't the sign to the start of a new chapter in my life, I don't know what is.

Every year from 11 December till 13 December, I relive my days, but now it seemed to be overwritten with happy celebrations of life. Life ended, but the new life must go on. It is still a sad day for me, but I choose to celebrate that my family lived and they live within me and in everything I do. Oh, how I enjoyed every moment of happiness. The next day, was my Hurdee night. It's the night before the wedding. It's a cleansing ceremony. Turmeric sticks are ground into a paste mixed with oil and smeared on the bride-to-be. Only ladies are allowed to apply this on to the bride or groom-to-be. At Schivan's home the same ceremony took place. Ma looked so happy and beautiful, she was also dolled up in her elegant sari's.

I loved my Ma so much. My adoptive parents were given an invitation. I know we did that personally so we wouldn't have that thrown in my face that they were not invited or given an invitation. If they wanted to attend, they would. I buried that there on that day. It was not my worry. In all of this planning I would hear 10 different versions from everyone involved, trying to make peace between me and my adoptive family. One person would say Schivan's family threatened them, another would say that I told them not to come. In all of this I just wished people would stop listening to everyone else.

My adoptive father's brother was overseas during this time, so it was understandable that he wasn't there. I had also personally invited my adoptive father's mum and she also didn't come. Neither did the so-called cousins I took as my own. But, the wedding went on with or without those I expected to be there.

Sadly, I still had it thrown in my face. I was reminded that they had taken me in as their own. How could I do this to them? I too took you as my own. I too loved you, spoiled you, bought you gifts, prayed for you, helped you when you had difficulties. But nobody heard that bit! Nobody heard my voice of what I did, I didn't want it broadcasted, like how you broadcasted my grave mistake to marry. They only hear your voice and why people should not attend my wedding, because my adoptive parents were not welcome. That was the wrong, the sin that I will never be forgiven for, by my family.

My wedding day arrived and I was nervous. I didn't want any drama on my wedding day. Again, I was told that if my "Mosi and Mosa" attended the wedding and caused a scene, they would be removed. I understood that Schivan had had enough and I also understand how my adoptive parents would feel if they'd be escorted out if they had to mention anything at the wedding.

I was stressed out.

I had helped my Ma's sisters get dressed. I did their hair and make-up, and I apologized that the hairdresser was not booked for them. Then it was time for me to get dressed. I looked stunning. My Ma's nephew drove me to the wedding hall. All the other cars followed and hooted as we entered.

It was happening.
I was getting married.
The butterflies and the adrenaline pumping.

I paused to think of my late family. It saddened me. As I've mention-ed, that over the previous 2 days, all those years ago in the year 1999, I had to lay them to rest on the same days. Years later I was getting married on the very same day, beginning a new life.

On my wedding day, I promised myself that I would make this new life about me. I promised I would be the happiest bride ever and I would not cry on my wedding day but display a beautiful smile. This chapter was about me and my happiness. Whoever wanted to be a part of it would be, and those who weren't could kindly exit.

Schivan had arrived, but we were not allowed to see each other just yet. There were a few welcoming rituals to be done for the boy's side.

And then it was time for me to walk down the aisle. I was led by a dhol (drum) and a clarinet player. They played an instrumental version of a wedding song. I smiled and waved as I saw friends and family, including work colleagues and our Kinross temple group. I was loved after all. Even after being told that nobody would attend my wedding because I excluded my adoptive parents. I was loved by many and those people gave me their blessings. I saw all these beautiful faces, some with tears in their eyes which brought tears to my eyes. For some sitting in the audience, I was that 12-year-old child they watched grow up. Some of those people had believed in me more than my blood. I did do a quick scan to see if my adoptive family were there.

I enjoyed my wedding day. I was both happy and sad, because I still wished that my adoptive parents and my siblings would walk through the doors. Sadly, it never happened. Again, in this happy moment, I blamed myself and believed that I had broken my family over my marriage. I never listened to them. I did things the way I felt was right and how it should be because it was my day. I blamed myself for not listening to my adoptive parents to marry a person they saw fit for me, instead of choosing the man I loved.

There was a friend of my adoptive father. He was more of a brother towards me and one day, when I lived with my Ma, she said I should get married to this man because he was older and rich. I was disgusted because this man was almost double my age. You know the line, "You rather marry an older man and be his darling than marry a young man and be his slave." I wanted to fall in love, not have an arranged marriage. I was also told that Schivan was so young and was asked how he would take care of me.

We were all young, but we grow up and become successful so why cut short something good just because an older man is richer? That rich man started at the bottom too. I do hope someday that man finds the love he deserves. After Schivan and I broke up, I formed a relationship with this man and even though he was nice and caring, I couldn't bring myself to have something with him. When he visited he would sneak into my room or me to his and we would cuddle and talk. Looking back at this, I am horribly disgusted with myself. I am not proud of many things I did, but I am glad I tried and experienced things so I could know myself better. I tried to form something that my adoptive parents and elder thought be perfect for me, but it was not. I tried, but sometimes what we are told by our parents and elders is just not meant to be and it can end up destroying a person.

I was in love with Schivan. I saw a life with him and I felt that connection. That is why I went against everyone. Yes, my adoptive parents wanted what was best for me, but not at the risk of my happiness. Had I married someone else, I know I would have had an affair to find love or I would have divorced. Standing up for this, for myself is what caused all my family relationships to break, because I stood with what I felt was right for me, and not just for the sake of making everyone happy. It was time to make myself happy.

Back to the wedding. The part to give your daughter away "kanyadhan" began, and my eldest aunt and uncle stood as my parents. I am sad to say they never wanted to do it, they were told to do it because nobody wanted to stand as a parent for me and Ma couldn't because she was a Widow (like I mentioned before, some things need to change. Regardless of Ma being a widow, she was still a mother to me). Had my Ma's brothers not put pressure on them to do this, nobody would have. Proud parents or not, thank you for playing a role in my upbringing.

All rituals were done. I was married and now Mrs. Ramdharee. We took our blessings from the priests and elders. There are always fun and games at our weddings as well as singing and dancing. Later, it was time to leave to my new home. Everyone cried as I had walked out and said my goodbyes. I felt heartsore for my Ma. Seeing her cry made me tear up too. My heart broke seeing her cry. She would always say, "My baby, why is everyone like this with you? They know you don't have parents but still they make you cry like this. I will look after you."

Ma,
I wish I could say I know you will be reading this.
I wanted to say this to the world so that the world will know how super my Ma was. No words will ever explain how much I appreciated everything you did for me. You were my rock. You filled my heart with so much love and hope. You gave me that hope that I could love again, and, more especially, live again. You took a damaged child and showered her with love even when your own didn't approve. Ma, I know that I always told you how much I loved you. Today I realize that telling you this didn't even come close to the unconditional love you showered upon me. Thank you for all of your blessing and prayers. Thank you for believing in me. Thank you for trusting me and, most importantly, thank you for being that pure form of a Mother

towards me. I wish there were more Mothers like you that could live forever and ever to shower those who need a mother's love.

I love you for always and always, for ever and ever.

Your loving Grand-daughter

As I said goodbye to everyone, I didn't shed a tear, though I felt extremely emotional when I saw Ma cry. I knew what she was feeling and why she was, and how her heart too, had ached for my late family and my adoptive family to be there.

I was happy to be married. Honestly, I was happier that I had left my family and was going into my new home. They were probably glad to be rid of this twit. Everyone said I was the first bride they hadn't seen cry. Maybe I was just so happy that this new chapter would be about me and not everyone else.

The celebrations continued at my in-laws' place in Standerton as they welcomed their new bride and daughter-in-law home. There were more gifts apart from all the wedding gifts. They had to still gift me things as a welcoming gift. I was so tired, I just wanted to sleep. I had spent all year planning for this wedding and it was finished in what felt like a split second. The next day was our reception and my family would have to come to collect me from my in-laws' home. After all the feasting was done, I was on the road again to my Ma's home to do the final ritual. When I got home, I changed into something comfy, as straight after we were boarding a flight to Cape Town for our honeymoon. As I got done, Ma came in to check on me. We had a moment together and told her how grateful I was to her and her brothers for making this a memorable moment for me. Ma explained that once the ritual was done, I couldn't look back and walk back into the house.

Schivan and his uncle were on their way to collect me. On their arrival, Ma greeted them and invited them inside for tea. Then it was time to leave. My bags were sent to the car and Ma collected a baby blue organza bag filled with rice grains, coins and notes. *That was to wish me well in my new home, may there always be food, good health, wealth and prosperity in my home.* As I stepped outside, Ma handed me the bag of grains and wished me well as a married lady. Before I left, it was the most heart-breaking thing for me to witness as a girl. My Ma wiped my feet with a clean handkerchief. *May the path you walk always be clear and blessed.* I cried as she did that. Ma was my elder.

In my culture, we touch the feet of our elders and ask for their blessings. To see my Ma bending over wiping my own feet, I cried. It felt so final that I was leaving my home. I left her home as a daughter and walked into another home as a daughter. It was almost like she was sending her daughter to my new family's home. She was asking them to look after me, or better than she had. We cried and I didn't want to let go. Ma said,
"Walk and don't look back."

Oh, I cried, even though I would come to visit as normal but this felt different. I got into the car and watched Ma wipe away her tears. Her wave slowly vanished out of my view. I was so blessed to have had all my Ma's brothers and sisters at my and Ma's side. A girl leaves her home to start a home of her own. She takes the name of her husband, she has to learn their ways of doing their prayers and giving her new family heirs to carry the name. Even though we are both Hindu and Hindi speaking our home prayers varied. I promised myself to be a good wife even though I didn't know what it was that a good wife does (*I still don't*). I just wanted to be like my mummy. As I watched her take care of us all, so too would I do, just as I had watched as a little girl. My heart ached because I wished mum was here to advise me. I wished my dad was there to tell my husband to never hurt me and to treasure me like my dad did.

It was a happy but sad drive to the airport. I was now a married woman. My honeymoon was amazing in Cape Town. We both did what we love best, and that's eating and looking for amazing food to tantalize our taste buds. We returned to Rustenburg after 2 weeks as we still needed to go back to Standerton to fetch our wedding gifts and clothes. We had roughly 700 guests at our wedding. Yip, a lot, I know.

Back in Rustenburg, it was time to unpack, and I had to start looking for a job. I was so used to working that sitting at home made me go insane. Living with my husband was a huge change for the both of us. I liked things a certain way and vice versa.

REFLECTION

We shouldn't be put into situations, where we need to choose between family and the one you love. Yes, your family wants only the best for you but you are also entitled to your happiness. It is not wrong to be putting yourself first, you should be priority!

14

IT'S NOT OVER

What marriage held for me would have to be between me and my husband and should it fall, I had no face to show because I walked out on all my family the day I became Mrs. Ramdharee.

My husband was now my priority. His family took me in as a daughter, they give me more love and respect then what was expected from my own blood. I am the eldest daughter-in-law in the Ramdharee home. When I was younger, I observed how couples fought and how marriages broke, how wives treated their husband's families and vice versa. How a wife treats her husband. I learnt what not to do in my own marriage. I would be different and I would share my time equally, be understanding, stand my ground and be firm. Nobody told or had taught me about marriage and especially how a wife should be. Honestly speaking, there is no such thing as a good husband or a good wife. There is no manual or instructions for marriage! You do you, darling. I had groomed myself for my future. I molded myself into who I wanted to be.

I am not perfect and neither is my husband. Over the years, you get influenced, or you adopt another person's characteristics. Over time I have learnt to just be myself. If I don't like it, I will say so.

I am always open with my husband, I tell him everything. He knows my bad habits and I know his. I will not hide anything from him. My reason for this is amongst us Indians, it typical that if a girl consumes alcohol or smokes, these "bad habits" mean we are loose, or no good for the "good boys". Being a married woman without sober habits, you are bound to be labelled by elders, family and haters. My husband knows I consume alcohol. I love wine and if anyone has something to say, go ahead because my husband doesn't mind having a wife that drinks. I've been told by many to tone down because it's so disgusting. Oh well. I don't care at all! That is just who I am.

My husband is my best friend and my strength. To some, my marriage seems too perfect but it's not. We have our ups and downs and we sort it out. We always make time to be with each other. We understand and care for one another. I couldn't have chosen a better life partner.

Schivan and I make the best of our marriage and, most importantly we respect each other's views. I will not go behind his back if he disapproves of something, and the same goes with him. A marriage shouldn't be where all your family members are in your business. Remember, you married each other not the entire family.

With the above set and that is how we saw, see and would like our marriage to go, it was not all a bed of roses and some of the above changed because it was not carved in stone. As we grow older, we change and so does life.

As a newly married couple, still learning how to tolerate and live with each other my marriage complications began. Well, you know that I have an issue calling anybody mum and dad.

A few months into my marriage, I was told that I needed to refer to my in-laws as mum and dad. The family insisted that I did, as it was the right thing to do. One comment stood out. I was told that *I should call my mother-in-law mum so she would feel comfortable around me.* Nobody should be forced to call someone mum and dad.

I love my in-laws, but I unfortunately cannot call them mum and dad. I sat my in-laws down and I told them to please forgive me but that I could not call them mum and dad. They understood that. However, it was so wrong in other people's eyes. Once again, other people's views should not matter. If my in-laws understood my feelings around this "mum, dad" thing then that's good enough.

I had asked my husband, if my parents were alive, would he have called my parents mum and dad. His response, "No! Why should I they are not my parents."

It is not right to assume that when a girl gets married, she will automatically call her in-laws' Mum and Dad. My point for not using the terms mum and dad, was because it was misused. People should understand, not everyone can utter those words. Respect that it is not a must. What should matter is that there is respect, love, peace and harmony in your new home. The first two years was off to a rocky start. We worked on one another's nerves. It was the simple things. I would get irritated, he would get into his car and drive off. We would say hurtful things to each other. I thought I made a mistake getting married, but we never gave up on us!

Some things are not set in stone. I grew up watching my mum and eldest aunt wake up early to prepare breakfast and lunch for the children and their spouses before we left for school or work. I grew up with that mentality that I also needed to wake up early to prepare food for my husband. The one morning I had woken early to prepare Schivan's lunch for work and to make him breakfast. He swore at me and sent me back to bed. He said that in this house there would be no such thing. We would make lunch for work the night before and put it in the fridge. There was no need for me to wake up extra early. And that was the last day I ever had to wake up early to prepare lunch for work.

I was questioned by family and friends as to why I never woke up to make a fresh meal for my hubby. Well, if my husband says no, it's no, and I will listen to him and nobody else.

Remember I resigned from my steady job in September 2014? I got married in the December of the same year. When my pension fund came through, I invested my pension fund, though I kept some money from there to pay off my car and a small amount for emergency purposes.

I found a job the January of 2015. I was employed for nine months, until their promises of making me permanent never materialized. To add to this, my work was constantly checked because some felt threatened. What took a lady 6 years to learn, I learnt in three months. I eventually resigned. I am worth more! I was unemployed for two years. During my time of unemployment, I tried to cook food to sell, just for extra money. I tried to keep myself busy and at least feel like I contributed to our home.

It was stressful because my husband had to support me, and I was going insane not working. I was so used to having my own money. In those two years, a lot had happened. Apart from marriage quarrels, my family had their fair share too.

My Ma was turning 70, so all Ma's children and grandchildren were added to a group chat. I had remained silent, just reading what was planned, until it surfaced that all the grandchildren should club in to pay for the DJ. My thought was that I didn't mind, but was this a party for youngsters or for Ma? Why was a DJ needed if it was only Ma's children and grandchildren? A decision was made that the grandchildren would assist in paying for the DJ. I told them that I was unemployed, and I could not assist financially. This is what had transpired from the group: the screenshots are under *Crucial Conversations*.

The conversation went on further between my eldest aunty and myself via SMS. This makes one realize, what I had said in the earlier chapters was indeed true. By this time, I was so furious. I sat in my prayer room and cried my heart out. Enough was enough. I had taken so much all these years and now this volcano named Alicia was going to erupt. I didn't care how it came out, but I was going to let off my steam to the person who rightfully deserved it.

Four lives were taken from me in a split second. I should be the last person to be ungrateful, but I guess my family would beg to differ.

After this so-called party episode, I had distanced myself from my maternal family but I still kept in contact and visited my Ma. I had the pleasure of having Ma come stay over on two occasions.

In the year 2017 I started a job on one of the mines in Rustenburg. I was grateful to have a job again.

On the second occasion, Ma was very sickly. After the last stroke, she couldn't walk properly. I would take her for walks to see the ducks, massage her and cook for her. I loved having Ma over, but that was the last time Ma visited because after that she just deteriorated.

Ma had to eventually live with my eldest aunt because she had another stoke. On one occasion, I called Ma to check on her as she had gone in for a check-up. She made me laugh. We were all concerned about her health. That was the most important thing, but to Ma her first words were, (Ma called me Di) she said, "Di, the doctor said I must wear only bedroom slippers. Di, what's going to happen to all my shoes Di? I can no longer wear them!" The way I laughed because she was worried that she couldn't wear her nice shoes. We had such good conversations every day. We would call each other until Ma had another stroke which took away her speech and movement to parts of her body.

She understood what I was saying but couldn't respond and my eldest aunty and I had another argument. She told me that I should stop calling and I was not welcome in her home to see Ma, that I must see her elsewhere. That elsewhere was either a family function or at my adoptive parents' home. Each child took turns in caring for Ma.

My adoptive parents and I were not on speaking terms and my husband was still not welcome in their home. My husband took me to see Ma when she visited Kinross or was admitted to hospital. She was in and out and her health worsened to a point of her relying on someone to bath, feed and take her to the loo. I know it frustrated her a lot because she was a very independent woman.

A call came through in July 2018, to say that the doctors could no longer do anything for Ma, and that we should just make her comfortable. I put aside all my issues I had with everyone, I put aside all the insulting remarks I got and we drove to my eldest aunt's house, not sure if she would allow me in because I was told that I was not welcome in her home. We were between Johannesburg and Rustenburg almost every third day and weekend. I started preparing myself for the worst. I was not going to be caught off guard. I played different scenarios in my head. I know I sound crazy, but that is the only way I know.

In early August, Ma's organs started to shut down, she became less responsive to our voices and she kept looking at the corner of the room and above her. We believe that when it's your time to pass on your ancestors and Lord Yamraj (God of death) sends his messengers to tell you so you prepare yourself. And He himself will collect you. You know, I always joked with Ma that the day when she receives all these messages she must tell me and I will fight with Lord Yamraj and tell him not to take her away because I need her. She can't leave me alone in this world. We would laugh and Ma would say, "Di, I can't wait to see my mother and father and your mummy, daddy, Tasha and Shivenn. I'll be reunited with my children"
Little did I know that this day was to be 10 August 2018.

My beautiful Ma took her last breath.

A few days prior to her passing, I went to visit Ma. Everyone took a break and I was keeping an eye on her. I told Ma, "Ma, I came to take you to Rustenburg today, I am taking you to get better. I am going to tell Mosi to pack a bag and we will take you with us." She looked at me, shook her head to say no, and lifted her hand towards me like when a person try's to shuu away a fly. I asked her, "Ma, are you leaving me?" She started to cry. I had such a huge bubble in my throat that day. I never shared this with anyone present that day, only with my husband because I cried my heart out as we drove back to Rustenburg. I told him, "Ma is going, she is leaving me." My Ma was going and as she had promised she would tell me, and she did.

Oh my heart, I cried and I told Lord Yamraj that I would put up a fight because he could not take my Ma. You only see Him when it's your time. But on the morning of 10 August 2018, he came into my dream and said, "I am taking Ma." I never thought anything of my dream until we received a message later that day, that Ma was no longer.

I couldn't cry. My tears wouldn't flow. I struggled to cry.
It felt weird, because everyone around me cried, but I couldn't, it hurt me on the inside. My Ma was gone to rest above with her beloved Angels.

When the hearse arrived, reality hit that Ma was dead. Reality hit me like a blow to the stomach, and those tears and hollow howls of grief filled the air around me.
Gosh, Ma was gone and I was once again alone.

My Ma, my mother, my person that showered me with unconditional love was gone.

Days went by and I felt empty. I tried to take my family responsibility leave at work, but the uncaring people there couldn't respect my mourning. They insisted I be at work. I refused because I was entitled family responsibility leave.

Before Ma passed away, I painted her nails. She chose silver. During that moment alone with her, I had also mentioned something to her. This something always troubled Ma and I know it gave her sleepless nights. To put her heart at ease, I told her that, I had finally received my father's pension fund money from the Department of Education, 19 years later. With the help of my dad's best friend Mr. Govender, we finally got it right. After countless submissions and proof of supporting documentation, the pension fund had finally paid out. Every time I had submitted documentation it got lost in their office. None of my parents' policies paid out. I had given up trying. I wonder how many more people out there have struggled to get policies and pension funds paid out. I've also been asked to bring the person that is deceased to provide proof of their policy. I give up.

My trust fund was R0.00. That is another mystery. All this troubled Ma a great deal because she had always asked and always pushed me to keep trying as it was money that was rightfully mine. I put her heart at ease, so if she had to go, she knew that her child had finally received what was rightfully mine.

With Ma laid to rest, I felt alone but I promised her that I would wear my Ramdharee surname with the same pride and importance as I did with my dad's surname.

Swami answered my prayers every time I sought comfort, though, I didn't only know Swami when I wanted something. No! I prayed through good and bad times.

I had still wished that my adoptive parents would see that Schivan was an awesome husband. I prayed every day that Swami would bring my family together.

It was just after my Ma's passing when my adoptive parents decided to visit Rustenburg with my other aunt, the middle one. I was excited. Could this be the moment I was waiting for? They had booked in somewhere and we visited them. Everyone got on, including with my husband. That night, all the children stayed over at my home. My adoptive parents apologized for not seeing this sooner and asked that we keep our relationship open for the sake of the children.

They even said that they could see that Schivan was a lovely person.

I could hear the angels and Ma singing in the heavens.
It had finally happened!

I forgave them for everything but I wouldn't forget and I would be extra cautious, just so that I did not get hurt again. With that relationship now under maintenance, I felt so good and, once again, Swami had made it work. I know things won't be how they should be, but at least we agreed to maintain the relationship.

Back to marital issues. As you know, long after marriage the newly married couple is expected to fall pregnant. That is what everyone believes should happen. When I was younger, in my early 20's, I really did want to have kids. I wanted to adopt children as well, but as time went on and my life seemed worse and I realized how everyone treated me, I was afraid that I would end up with someone who wanted kids and didn't care about how I felt. I had changed my mind about having children. I can already hear your disappointment and the name calling.

Schivan had the same feeling. He also didn't want children. We spoke about it when we started dating. We felt the same about not having children. We love children, don't get us wrong, but to have our own or to adopt was just not for us. Yes, I know, me of all people should know how important it is, and I was an orphan. I should know. We agreed that, should either of us have a change of heart, we would speak up. Years went by and we felt the same. We got married and we had more pressure on us to conceive, despite us not wanting children and saying we didn't want children.

Everyone was just waiting for us to have a baby, not worried if we are happy, or if we were ready. No, you must have a baby. We want grandchildren, we want nieces and nephews, and you are getting old. The pressure became so unbearable. I cried to Schivan on so many occasions and asked him, does our happiness and what we want not matter? Schivan always says I take things to heart and I should just take it with a pinch of salt. I tried that, but he didn't understand that being a woman meant that all eyes were on me.

Trust me when I say, having a baby *does not define my womanhood*. I have breasts, I have a vagina, I get my periods and I have a healthy sex life. Why should bringing a child into this sick world decide if I am woman enough? The Answers: So that there is someone to carry the Ramdharee name! When you get old you will regret not having kids! You will grow old alone! Kids complete you! Children are a blessing! I can go on.

Yes, I agree with everything said, but is that not up to me and my husband as a couple to decide? Why must it be family and friends making huge decisions in our life? If you want to have a baby, please go ahead but stop begging others to do the same. Respect their decisions.

When we visited family, especially my husband's side, I was always questioned about when I was going to have a baby, when the grandchild was coming. I was told I needed to make my in-laws grandparents, to complete their life. I would tell them that Schivan and I didn't want children.

I would hear: that I am selfish for not conceiving,
I am not woman enough if I don't have a child,
I am going against my husband's wishes,
He wants a child and I am not giving him a child,
I am cold hearted,
I should stop the pill without my husband knowing to fall pregnant,
I am abnormal for not wanting to be a mum.

Those kinds of words hurt me more than you can imagine, and to think they were coming from other women, women that should know how hard it is to bring up a child, the importance of respect to your partner and the troubles we have as a lady to conceive. I dreaded every trip to a family function or family. Yes, I was the daughter-in-law but bearing a child was between me and my husband.

I started becoming depressed because of all the pressure. It upset me that we were not seen or listened to about this issue. He didn't want children because we struggled to keep ourselves safe in this world, and he didn't want to bring an innocent life into the cruelty we saw. He was also concerned about his work hours and the cost of living, which only rises. I agreed with him fully. He was not prepared to put us in debt just to give our child a better life. Our grandparents did that, our parents did that. Should we just pop babies because we were told?

Everyone says things will fall into place, don't worry about money. That everyone wasn't in my home 24/7 to see how we scraped through the month between the two of us. That everyone didn't see that we started work at 5am. That everyone didn't see a tired man and woman coming home from a long day at work. Nobody saw the days when I was in pain that meant I couldn't walk from my bed to the bathroom.

We live a happy life, with no stress. We go as we please, sleep when we want, we have a carefree life and we enjoy that. I feel that if a couple is happy, just let them be. As husband and wife, having a baby is their decision.

Schivan was told he isn't a man if he doesn't have a child. Almost every rotten thing in this world has a stigma attached to it, if you don't have a label then you are judged by people who have no right judging you because they are not perfect. If God wants me to have a child regardless of our decision, He will make it happen. I have full faith in that, but for as long as I say no and it doesn't happen, I am the driver of my life and God has written my path, not you.

If you have understood what I have written here, then you will have an understanding of why I choose not to have children. People have taken it upon themselves to try and change my mind,
"Have a baby, the baby will heal you, and you will be an awesome mum."

I had the greatest opportunity, raising my cousins and my new younger brother and sister. When I had my brother and sister from my adoptive parents taken away from me again, it caused pain and depression.

What I went through as a child at the tender age of 12, created a fear in me for if my child may have to live alone without us. What if we die before they are old enough? I have so much fear that it stops me. Yes, I know, fear holds us back, but you have no idea how I feel on the inside for you to say "have a baby".

Call me cold, but I don't even get broody. I can give my love to millions so that nobody ever feels alone. I can generate that much love, because I have felt what some will only feel in their 40's, or 50's. I cannot give anyone a child. I had to always think about others happiness.

The day I got married, that was my happiness, it was time for me. I became important and a priority alongside my husband.

I wish people would see that it wasn't an easy life for me. Now is my time for me to enjoy my life as I please. I have been through so much that at least show that respect to me and grant me that last bit of 30 years to enjoy being with my husband and my fur babies. To those that say I am not a mother because I have not birthed a child. I am a mother and Schivan is a father. We have two fur babies. Kiara and Chloe complete our lives. I am a mother to many, just look deeper. We are happy being like this. Accept it. If you know us well enough, you will see the love we have for children even though we still stand firm in our decision. I admire people who have children. You are doing an *excellent* job.

I came across this on a meme: When people saw a barren woman in Sarah, God saw the mother of all nations. When people saw a poor young shepherd in David, God saw a mighty King of Israel. When people saw a poor prisoner in Joseph, God saw a powerful Minister in Egypt. So never mind what people see in you. God has a perfect plan for you.

Likewise, God has a perfect plan for me.

As this "child bearing phase" amongst the family was going on, we started distancing ourselves from everyone because it became annoying. What added to our decision going forward was that my health took a nose dive after Ma's passing. I was suffering and I still suffer with my back, feet and groin. The pain became unbearable, and it didn't stop. It started in 2016 and it just got worse to a point of being unable to walk properly, I had to literally hold onto something to stand up or to take a few steps. My feet were extremely painful, every step was awful. I wondered how I had ended up here, and if this was going to be forever.

We went from doctor to doctor and all my tests came back clear. Some of the doctors told me it was all in my head.

Finally, we got a diagnosis on my back. The disc in my lower back was narrowing, hence the pain, and the arch on my feet had collapsed, causing me to have flat feet. My husband vowed he would find someone to fix me, and he did. He found a Bio-kineticist in Rustenburg. This lady was magic.

She assessed me and I started going to gym four times a week and doing G5 treatments once a week for a month. If I tell you that she could not touch my feet with one finger you would not believe me. That is how sore my feet were. There were many sessions where I had given up and cried my eyes out because I would be fine for a few days and then the pain would appear out of nowhere. For a year, I stuck to this routine and I was functioning like myself again. She was able to apply so much pressure to my feet, that it felt good to have feet again. I still suffer a lot with my lower back and feet. I try to keep up with exercise at least twice a week. I don't want to be where I was in 2017.

Still, the groin pains got worse and my period pains were out of this world. Once again, we were back and forth between doctors and again I had to deal with doctors, even though some were female!

"Oh man, your period pains can't be that bad."
"I had worse pains than you."
"Once you have a baby this will be a thing of the past."
"The pain is in your head."
"Have a baby."

We had exhausted our medical aid trying to find out what was wrong with me. Thanks to the change in my GP, and her expert skill, she got to the bottom of it and referred me to her Gynecologist. On my arrival at the gynae, I was extremely nervous. He did a transvaginal scan and what do you know? We had found the root cause that had also added to my back pains. To the doctors that said that it's in my head, my gynae had found that I had fibroids and endometriosis in my uterus.

I had to undergo a laparoscopy and have the endometriosis and fibroids removed. Although after having my uterus cleaned and my gynae telling me I was clean and could conceive, I opted for an IUD (Intrauterine device). Some months it's a breeze and pain free and some months I suffer that I am unable to walk due to ovarian cysts. I have never given birth but I sure feel like I am in labor and something is coming out of my vagina. (Too much info here but this pain is real.) I've had females question period pain and cyst pain. Well, here we go. This pain isn't overrated because when it arrives, it catches you off guard. You are in so much pain you don't know if you need to urinate or poo, or to take a hot shower or bang your head against a wall. With all this pain, having a child would not solve this and it isn't the solution. I know women who have had children and still suffer a great deal.

With all this, it added to our decision to not have children at any cost because my husband knows how I suffer and I am left drained and cannot function properly on most days. That is the part family, friends and outsiders don't see in our home. No matter how many smiles I put on on a daily basis, you will never know because I am probably highly medicated to prevent you from seeing my agony. Those masks came off as soon as I get home because that is where I can be me. So, every time you have asked us when the baby is coming, or why are there no babies yet, please know that we have decided not to. I have my pain free days to celebrate, because if I had a child, that poor child would have an absent mother because she is constantly in pain. I don't have the energy for it. Let me be, let us be. We are happy as we are. Who knows, maybe this decision was made for a reason that saved us both heartache of failed pregnancies? God knows his plan for us.

With this part below please don't get the wrong idea of my husband, he is an amazing man that will fight tooth and nail for me. This was just a phase and it was corrected.

Being sick did take a toll on my marriage as well. I was on some hectic medication at some point. One night, while being so highly medicated I remember he mentioned I should go to bed because my meds were kicking in. I refused. I mean it was my body and I knew when I was sleepy. He mumbled something and I threw the television remote on the floor. From behind me, like the back of the couch he grabbed me and started shaking me and throwing these light, mini punches on my back. They were not hard punches it was more like a tap but consistent. I eventually told him to stop and he went back to the kitchen. I sat in the lounge and cried. What had just happened?

He just shook me up. I was wrong to throw the remote. I know I can be a bit much at times.

The next day I woke up at 04:00 for work. I left home at 05:00 every day to be at work by 06:00. It was extremely tiring for me. The people I worked with never understood my pain levels and why I limped or sat in one spot with my hot water bottle even on the hottest days. I had to work because it's what we do to live comfortably and the extra salary helped a lot. My day ended at 15:00.

Tired and dreading going home as I didn't get much sleep and I was trying to make sense of the previous night, I was moody and this guy on the highway was hogging traffic. I came out onto the left lane and overtook him to get into the right lane in front of him. As I did that, I swore at him and told him to drive in the left lane. As the road joins to become one lane, this man drove onto the yellow line on my left-hand side and side swiped my left mirror and door. Now I was furious. I floored my Bantam bakkie and made him pull over. He did so and I asked him what his problem was. I told him he had just side-swiped me and that I needed a photo of his ID and for him to follow me to the police station. Well, this man started swearing at me, saying things like "Jou ma se…" you get the idea. Did he just swear about my mother? Oh hell no. His car looked like he was in a lot of accidents. He got into his car and drove off. There was no way that I was going to allow this guy to drive off. I followed him like a Formula1 driver and, even in my shaken state, managed to get a photo of his car. He tried to lose me in the residential areas, but I kept on him.

Eventually I managed to pull up next to him at a traffic light and get a good look at him. He was definitely on something, or deranged. I had a nail appointment that I didn't want to miss. It always made me happy, so I just said, "Swami I leave it to you."

When I stopped in the parking lot of the nail salon, I went to assess the damage. It was so bad. By this time, the adrenaline was wearing off and I was feeling weak and sick. Schivan was not talking to me because of our fight. I was wrong to throw the remote. I know sometimes I do go overboard. I sent him a picture of the door and mirror. He responded with, "You want to be an independent woman isn't? I'll send you the insurance number. Call them and sort it out."

I hadn't even explained that I was in an accident. I was shaken up pretty bad because I'd never been in a car accident before. After reading his message, I made my mind up that I wouldn't go home that night. Had this been his sister or mum he would have called and been there in a heartbeat.

That day, my husband broke my spirit. I hit rock bottom and I regretted marring him because of the way he treated me. It took me back to an argument we had while dating. He told me that his family would always come first, and then me. That day, I realized I was nothing to this man. I called a friend and her husband was there in 10 minutes and she arrived shortly after. I cried and told her everything that had happened and Schivan's response. I got my nails done and then drove to my friend's house and calmed down. I told them that I didn't want to go home. It was already 18:00 and my husband didn't even call to check why was I not at home, or to ask if I was ok. I refused to call or go home. I always kept extra money in case, at some point I needed to book into a hotel. It was moments like this that I was grateful that I saved money for an emergency.

We went to the police station, I handed over all the information and wrote down everything as it had happened. It was now 20:00 and my husband still had not checked on me. His cousin at that time was living with us and he had called, "Sister, where are you? It's late and you are not at home. Are you ok?" I explained everything and he was furious with Schivan for not even checking up on me. Finally, around 20:30, Schivan and his cousin pitched up at the police station. I couldn't look him in the eye. I lost all respect for him that day.

We all went to a restaurant to eat and allow Schivan and I to talk in a neutral venue. I didn't have much to say to him, just the utter disgust I had. I ended up going home and I didn't even want him to touch me. Over the weekend, he arranged for the repairs and insurance claims for the damages and the photo of the man's car so that they could track him down. I had no feelings towards my husband that day, I was just blank. We discussed what had happened. All he could say was, "I thought someone opened their car door on your door, so it was no biggy." Then I let loose. "No biggy? That's why you didn't call to check why I was not at home? Do you have any idea how you have made me feel?

I am not your wife if this is how you want to treat me!
I am not a mat that can be stepped on and off as you please!
You are no better than my family.

I didn't expect this from you! Now I know that I am not a priority and I am not family because family comes first. But not when I need you! I deserve respect from you! You better tell your father that you raised your hand to me and that you left me to fend for myself because of your ego!" I worried about who I had married because he had told me once, in an argument, that he only has one mum and one dad and they can't be replaced but I, his wife can be replaced by another. That is why I have no priority. I am glad that over these years, these words have been taken back and I hope that I am a priority alongside the importance of his family, because I left my home for him.

I truly admire a man that makes his wife his world and is not scared to show the world how much he loves her.

When he raised his hand, to him he didn't hit me because I wasn't injured. But regardless, he raised a hand to me and made contact. That day he put fear into me, fear that he would do it again. He never said sorry. There was no apology, just a promise that he would try harder. Years later, he feels terrible for the way he treated me in the first 3 years of our marriage.

I would like to think this was the worst. We argued a few more times after this and he would drive off, bang the cupboards or yell out that he wished he was dead, or could God not take him now. It had always upset me when he would do this. It was so uncomfortable to not talk to each other after these arguments. One of the things we had decided on was that whenever we argued, we would never go to bed angry. We would talk about what upset us and find a solution. We have both calmed down a lot with age and understanding.

Schivan never understood my grief and the emotional side to my life and it irritated him. He had never experienced what I had gone through until one day I decided I would explain everything and how I felt. I think that was the best thing I could do. It not only made him understand me better, but our arguments lessened. I do feel that, the majority of the time, it is me who starts it and that is because he either went and changed our plans and agreed with something his dad had decided, it wasn't run by me or something was discussed by everyone and he didn't update me on it. That's how the fights started. He has never picked a fight first, to be honest. He never found, till this day, something to complain about. He isn't that person who will shout at me if I haven't cooked supper, or if I haven't cleaned. He will make a plan or rather serve me supper. My husband cleans up, he cooks and helps me around the house. Although sometimes he does tick me off.

My marriage isn't perfect. We work on *us* to better our marriage.

Some time ago, he mentioned to me that he realized he was wrong on many occasions, one of them when he was too hard on me and expecting me to just accept that it was his way or no way. A typical example was me not keeping my father's surname. He refused point blank that I not keep it, not even a double barrel. Today he says, "There are a lot of things I shouldn't have done to you."

Men and boys, if you can't stand to see your sisters, mothers or daughters being ill-treated, don't do it to another female or your spouse. What we have learnt thus far as a couple, is that it's good to have open communication, it's good to get some space and sort it out with a cool head. Space does make you realize what you have taken for granted.

We are in this marriage together. Schivan and I have come a long way. Despite our heated arguments, we have worked through it and we love each other. We are six years into our marriage and counting.

He reminds me a lot of my father, especially his short temper and the way he loves to spoil me and do things for me. I admired my parents' love for each other. It's not about the material things and expensive gifts, it's moments such as him going to the shop to buy bread and coming back with my favorite chocolates. It's about the small things that make you go "aw" and all puppy dog eyes. I love him and I look forward to many more years with him.

In June 2019 my husband got extremely sick. His diagnosis was septicemia. The day I was diagnosed with endometriosis he was at home, sick. He was on and off with a fever and it was very odd for Schivan to be sick. When he was sick, it was not at all good. That very day, I made an appointment with our GP for him to get checked. The doctor ran blood tests and we were waiting for the results. That night, my husband was shivering and absolutely hot. It was the middle of the night and this man was sick. I was willing to rush him to the ER. His phone rang nonstop and, I mean, it was the middle of the night, so I decided to answer it. It was our GP with his blood results. She flagged it as urgent and as soon as she received the report, she called.

She said,
"Get your husband to the ER now. I have arranged for the doctor on call to attend to him just get him to the ER immediately."

I helped him to the car and I drove like a mad woman to the ER. The doctor on call was waiting, and my GP kept on checking in with me to see how things were. I take my hat off to the doctor. Your service that day was nothing I have ever seen in my days of having a GP. Thank you.

Another round of tests was done. It was now 03:00 and I called in at work to say I would not be in as I had a family emergency. Schivan's tests came back with a positive check for septicemia. To date, we don't know how all this happened. Calls were made and he was taken into high care. I put on my strong face for him, to show I was not at all scared. I knew if he saw me worried, he would not focus on himself. I asked him if should call his parents and he said I should call them later, not at that stage. We didn't want to create panic.

As they wheeled him off to high care, I walked out the ER in tears. I sat in my car at 03:00 that morning and howled. I prayed for his health and that he be ok. I drove home. I couldn't sleep, so I called his father and told him that they needed to come to Rustenburg, that Schivan was in high care. My in-laws are God sent. Yes, there are things I don't agree with, but they have never insulted me.

They have only ever given me love. I called up Schivan's uncle and aunt that stay a few kilometers away from us. This aunty and uncle are like our parents, here in Rustenburg. I am forever grateful to have them close by. Thank you, Kaki and Kaka, (Kaka is what you call your fathers brother and Kaki is what you would call his wife) for everything that you do for me and Schivan. I packed a bag for Schivan and I was at the hospital, anxiously waiting to see him.

I sat at his bedside watching his heart rate spike then drop. It was the same with his temperature. All I did was pray for my husband's wellbeing. I was at ease when everyone arrived and I was not alone to go through this. It was hard to eat. All I could think was, "Swami, don't take another person I love away from me. Swami, you need to heal him."

I know I was being negative. I tried to be positive, but I was scared that this could go either way. Our GP kept checking in and I sent her every update. She at one point said that if we needed anything, I was to call her. Bless you in abundance, Doctor.

By the third day, Schivan was starting respond positively to the medication and began to eat. He looked so much better. The doctors moved him to the general ward and he was discharged 2 days later. Thank you, Swami, and everyone that said a healing prayer for my family during this time. Thank you.

With all these highs and lows, I am so glad that I never gave up. My husband and I never gave up on each other and the people who loved and supported us were always around. I am grateful for all this. Sometimes when the only thing you know how to do is to be strong, then strong it is.

We learn from so much. My marriage is better than ever, and I wouldn't want it any other way. We have both grown and changed and learnt to adapt to one another. Yes, we do have our occasional arguments but it's definitely not as bad as the first 3 years.

Marriage is what you make of it. You need to have respect for each other. You need to talk about those fights. You have to compromise and meet each other halfway. That understanding needs to happen. My marriage isn't perfect but we have corrected those imperfect things. We don't go to bed angry. We say what needs to be said, and get over it.

Understand that both your upbringings were different, you can't expect him to chew the chicken bone the way you do because that's how you were taught to eat it!

Agree, as a couple, what is best for you, not just because it's carried from generation to generation, and it *must* be done like this. Do it, but within your means and be realistic.

It's not what everyone wants, it's between you and your spouse. It's ok to say no and it's ok to be happy for you and your home, not everyone else. Your happiness matters!

I would marry Schivan again in every lifetime. I don't regret marrying him.

REFLECTION

Marriage is what you make of it. Choose to talk about your arguments instead of letting them be. Communication is so important between husband and wife. Decisions that need to be made should involve husband and wife. In this day and age, you need to think realistically and not be pressurized just because it has been done from generation to generation.

15

TELLING THE WORLD

I have only ever told school classmates and a few work colleagues my story, and that was only if I felt pulled to do so. In many instances, the person I was telling needed to hear that story. It motivated them to go on. I never thought to share it with the world. I started writing in 2006, but I never thought I would finish this story, to share it. It was more of a reminder to myself about everything and to see how far I have come. Whenever I felt pain, I would write a little, then I would stop for some time and start again. Eventually I gave up. Maybe it wasn't such a good idea. But, between the years of 2015 and 2019, my urge to create Suicide Awareness and to beak boundaries, grew stronger.

On 11 December 2015, it was my parent's death day. Before I could wake up that morning, I heard Swami's voice. I kept hearing this voice, and the voice kept saying
"Share your story to the world."
He said,
"It is time to tell your story to the world."
Was I going crazy? I was supposed to share my story to the world? Like, seriously, that's a lot of people. I woke up and I told Schivan that this is what Swami said I needed to do. So, on my family's 16th death Anniversary, I went onto Facebook and I typed out what I had

held back for the past 16 years of my life. I shared about the day I lost my family to a murder-suicide.

I didn't think anything of it at first, as I was just following the instructions I was given. I shared my story. There was an outpouring of comments and sharing. Friends that I schooled with were in awe because they never knew that I went through this tragedy. I never broadcasted this to just anyone. I told people that needed to hear it. Teachers that taught me in school had reacted the same, as they never knew. I was always smiling and bubbly. But this story wasn't shared so that I could get to hear wonderful things about myself. It was shared because this time it wasn't about one person hearing my story, I was telling it for the first time, to the world on a social media platform.

I let it be and allowed what needed to take course. In the December of 2016, I was contacted by a local newspaper to do a piece for the 16 Days of Activism against Gender Based Violence. My story was being viewed by many by this time.

That brings me to 2 years later. In December of 2018, I made my first video and posted it on Facebook, to create Suicide Awareness. Once again, I felt this drive that I must do it. I must make this video. I followed my heart, and I did it. This time, it was definitely viewed by the world. Messages poured in from Texas, Australia, New Zealand, Canada, Africa, my list can go on. That video is still on social media, changing lives. I say this because, apart from being such an inspiration to the many that I have touched, it has saved lives. My mission in life is to save a life. I am not doing this for fame. I am doing this because I want victims and survivors of suicide to know that they are loved and they matter, that suicide isn't a solution, it is not the way to go.

I finally saw the light and I realized this is what Swami wants me to do. This is what my reason for staying behind was. I was left behind to tell this story to the world, of how an orphan survived. Of how life can be so cruel, but at the same time, beautiful beyond measure. Messages had come in to create a group to help people cope. This is my passion, to create Suicide Awareness.

It was in May 2019 that Surviving Suicide was born. This is my very own Suicide Awareness support group for Victims of Suicide, Survivors of Suicide and for people that have lost loved ones to Suicide. I call them warriors, because a warrior fights on.
My story has saved lives, it has stopped suicide attempts and given warriors hope and strength to go on.

You are not alone.

There have been columns written for magazines, newspapers, radio and television interviews. I had extremely good feedback, except for the first time I was interviewed for TV. It was a pre-recording. I did the video at home and the guys in the studio did the rest. I never got backlash from the many I inspire, but I got a backlash from family. They had focused more on me stating that my mother could have had an affair. But with this stated on national TV, I had also mentioned that there could be other things such as financial issues or stress. My family chose to focus on the affair part. My mother's two sisters were upset, and my adoptive father was angry at me for slandering my mother on TV. After that episode, my adoptive father's sister had also decided to have a go at me on social media and she attacked me on someone else's post. The screen shots are under "*Crucial Conversations*".

My family may take offence to the below.

Bringing up my mother's affair was not something new to me. How is it that different people with no relation had something to say about my mother's affair?

It started when we had visited a psychic medium I was in my 20's and it was a burning question on all of my aunts lips. At that age I had not known of this, but overhearing it made me question if this was true or not. The years went by and I would secretly overhear my aunts talk amongst themselves.

When I started my Suicide Awareness video in 2018, one of my dad's students had made contact with me through social media.

"I am so glad that I found you, to see that you are ok and grown up into such a beautiful young lady. But there is something I should tell you as it has been killing my conscience and I feel it's only right to tell you this and to finally get it off my chest."

I knew this student, as he was one of the schoolboys that came home and my father was fond of. These boys were like brothers in my eyes. I was willing to hear him out. He started off by telling me how sorry he was and that he did try his best to stop what he was about to say and since my family's passing, he has never uttered a word and it has been eating him up on the inside. He went on to say, he had found out about his "friend's relationship" with my mum. He had told his friend to stop it and end things with my mother because my father was their teacher and they all looked up to my dad, my dad was their father figure, and it was wrong.

According to this "boy", his friend had agreed to stop the relationship with my mother. Only for him to find out that it didn't end. They had tried to stop it, my dad found out and things went the way they did. He apologized to me and said that he had kept this from me for so long as he couldn't locate me. That was the second time I had heard of my mum's affair. The third occasion was just before my wedding when I was inviting my father's side of the family for my wedding and my Kaki had also brought the "affair" part up when we spoke.

She had mentioned that they had met with the police and they had found letters between my mother and this "boy" and her diary entries found in her diary confirmed it. The fourth time was when I went to Durban to invite my paternal grandmother for my wedding and when I gave her my wedding invitation, her words were, "Don't be like your mother and be with other men, look after your marriage!" The fifth time I heard about it was from another student of my father's when I had asked him straight out if what I had heard thus far was true. "Unfortunately, it is true", he said.

After all of these instances, when I questioned my Aunts, all I heard was
"that isn't true",
"your mother was not that kind of a lady",
"how can you think that of your mother?"

To me it really did not matter if my mother did have a relationship with this "boy". I am in no way embarrassed, neither do I think any less of my mother, however I do feel ashamed to associate myself with people that lie and fail to tell the truth to my face. I was asked how I could believe a stranger's words and not that of my family. What truth have you given me to even trust your word? Even if this affair statement is just an assumption, let it be. I don't hold anything against my mother, and I am still proud of my mum. After all, she is my mother. I wouldn't let a so-called "affair" change the way I feel towards my mum. So, there. I have said it! Something that some people still wish not to talk about because talking about things like infidelity, suicide and so much more are to be hushed and swept under the rug, because of "What would people say?"

Between my mum, dad and this boy only they will know what transpired and how it all began and ended. And to that dear boy…

Dear Boy,

It's sad that I do know who you are as you were in our home daily. We played Carrom board and chess together. At first when I heard of this, I was angry for what had transpired between you and my Mum. Yes, it does take two to tango and this was wrong for both parties. I want you to know that I have forgiven you but I won't forget. If you are reading my book, I wish to meet you. There was a time when I did want to run you over if I ever saw you when I was visiting Durban, but I am past that phase now!

I don't want to "moer (hit) you." I just want to look at your face and ask you, "How have you lived with this since my family's passing?" I want to know if your mind is at peace. I know this was not easy for you. This is me reaching out to you. You are the missing link to me finding complete closure to this tragedy.

You know what's sad about this entire thing? It still boils down to unanswered questions. I know many will tell me to just leave it! Stop digging, it's best I don't know. In many suicide cases, the survivors are left to pick up the shattered pieces and we try to make sense of it all. If this can complete my search, and answer my questions then I have closed that loop and found closure for myself. I know this tragedy was hard and an emotional roller coaster for both maternal and paternal families. I just wish there was transparency and the truth told to me from day one, I do have every right to know. I know that some would rather turn a blind eye to the truth because "the truth is a bitter pill to swallow", but it didn't help me to do that.

You know, I understand I opened old wounds for my adoptive mother and her sisters. Again, when is the right time to speak about taboo subjects. We can't stay scared of what others will say.

I was told I should not have even mentioned it, because now everyone would start gossiping again and I gave everyone something to talk about. It was okay for me, all these years to say that my father murdered my mother and siblings and then tragically took his own life but it was not ok to mention my mother and her affair. Some believed I had lost the plot and was using my story as a show.

I do not sugar coat or hide anything. I have said it before and I will say it again. I am not at all embarrassed to tell the world that my mother had an affair, that my father murdered my family, that my

247

father killed himself. All these stigmas and what we can and can't talk about need to STOP. I guess my dad took their lives and his, because of the very same stigma. It is time for us to stop this!

This is why people do not talk about things. It's because of people that are quick to judge and label. We must choose what we talk about. A rape victim must not speak up, an abused man, woman or child must stay quiet because we are worried that family ties will break or too many people will talk. Where do we draw the line on stigma's and telling the truth? Stop sweeping things under the rug, to hush it up.

What is next for me? Getting this book published. This book holds many untold truths. Things that even the people who think they are the greatest things ever to walk this earth, will read. It is raw and seen through my eyes. For those that see it from the different views of my maternal family, please write your own book. This is not to justify who is right and wrong in the life that I lead or led before. I am writing this to show you what I saw my life as, growing up and my version of aging beautifully into life.

I appreciated all the hardships, heartache and joy.
I know this book will make many bitter mouths and sour faces but it's not about me being liked by everyone. I am not everyone's cup of tea. I am a survivor and I hope my story helps those contemplating suicide. I hope you can grasp something from here.

This story isn't over;
Talk about what you are going through. There shouldn't be any lid on it!

We need more people to talk about what they are going through so we can help them through this obstacle course. How do we help others if we too are scared to speak up? I have no cap on my mouth and I am transparent. Family members cannot talk amongst themselves for fear of gossip, and they are too scared of who will get to know what they share. On so many occasions, I was so scared to speak out to family, but I found comfort in talking to friends and even, sometimes, strangers.

Stop judging and start helping.

It became too emotional at one stage, but after all the above, I had the feeling to go ahead and start writing again. In January 2019, I had decided to go full steam ahead in writing this book. I pushed myself to write something every day. Even if it was just one line! It was emotionally draining because I had to relive everything. Today, this book is completed because of the determination of trying to save a life and to create Suicide awareness in South Africa. Through this adventure, my family, friends, and dear husband stood by me and encouraged me every step of the way. But it was not only the above people. The world stood by me on social media, by helping me spread the word that suicide is not the way to go!

This is my purpose and my calling and I will carry it through.

REFLECTION

We never realize why we go through the things we do. I was spared so that this story could be told. It carries a powerful message to show you that, you are needed and loved. Don't give up! Life is breathtakingly beautiful. Live it to its fullest.

16

SWAMI AND HIS DIVINE LOVE

As a young one, yes, I prayed as my parents taught me to. We observed our fasts which were strictly vegetarian meals and no pork and beef. I knew there was a supreme being, I knew of other religions, I had also asked questions to educate myself, as everyone has their own beliefs. Growing up in a Hindu home, I am glad that my parents brought us up to respect other religions and that I carried with me.

After my parents passing, I turned to God more than ever for guidance, and flooded the heavens with questions. I have found myself losing my spiritual path at certain times. At some point, I gave up on prayer.

I went cold turkey on prayer and refused to believe in it because if there was someone up there in the heavens, they would not allow me to go through such pain and tragedy, knowing a child needs their parents. I cried and begged at prayer altars and in our home, prayer rooms or even while I tried falling asleep. I cussed out to the man above. People around me had their own view about my religion and took it upon themselves to insult me and tell me that I worshiped a devil religion. Remember, I was still finding myself in this world and I had to also find my spiritual path again.

As much as I was angry with God, I realized that I need that higher being to intervene. I found Swami "Sri Sathya Sai Baba". One day, a classmate asked me who I follow and I said that,

"I follow the teaching of Sri Sathya Sai Baba".

Her response amused me,

"Then you are sold to the devil."

I was so disgusted. If I do not follow *your* religion, it does not mean that my religion is the work of the devil. I found peace and Divine love in his teachings and from day one of accepting and taking that first step, I have full faith in the one in whom I trust. This is the same as any other person who believes in their religion. Now, I am not here to preach and change you to Hinduism. I just want to say that whatever and whoever you believe in, pray to or even if it's nothing. Have faith in what you have faith in.

Swami says,

"When you take one step towards me, I will take ten steps towards you." I did that and I found my place. With Swami's guided teachings, he teaches you to just be a better you in whatever belief you are in. Love all Serve all.

When I lived in Kinross, I joined the Sai Centre there and oh, what a moving experience it was. I would dream endlessly about Swami, I would sit at his feet in his Ashram and talk. He would give me Vibuthi (Holy ashes). I did have fights with Swami too, especially when things where upside down. I prayed the hardest when it was time for results and report cards. I blamed Swami for my parents' deaths and for keeping me alive. Then, when things went well, I prayed again and when it didn't, I didn't bother. Until one day, when I decided that if I am here and there is a purpose, Swami will get me through this. I can't be angry with him. I allowed prayer and Swami back into my life and, once again, it felt good to pray. This time, even in the bad, I prayed in the good I prayed, and I thanked Swami for everything, every day. With everything that went wrong, there was a lesson learnt and I thanked Swami for that. Today I am here, spreading love and hope because of Swami. Swami was with me through all my highs and lows, even though I ditched him, but he never ditched me. I am forever grateful for his Divine love. Afterall, I had even met my husband while doing Seva (service to mankind) Swami's work. What else could I ask for?

Apart from my love for Swami, I was graced with the presence of Archangels. I am not sure if you believe in Archangels. Well, if you do, this will make sense.

Since this dream, my life's perspective has been changed. It had given me hope that I would heal my wounds and I truly believe what I saw in my dream was a mirror image of my damaged soul. Oh, and I do believe in Angels.

I had a beautiful dream, some years ago, about Archangels Raphael and Michael. In this dream, they had come to earth to meet me. Big, bright and beautiful. Mind you, at that time I knew nothing about "angels" let alone their names. I knew they had wings and were created by God. In this dream, as they descended, the light was getting brighter than a Super Moon. Their energy around them was intense. Wings!

This is still an understatement. Nothing can describe their wings.

Their wings were magnificently beautiful, white, pure and bright. The wingspan alone was beyond breath taking. Their glow was blinding. It was like nothing that I have ever seen before. Not even the movie angels come close. They were giants as I stood in between their feet, gazing up at them. They were tall and muscular, I felt warm and protected around them. I was in awe.

I am open to all religions and I believe no matter who we pray to, it's all the same. We all pray for love, peace and protection and no religion is better than the next. The Archangels began speaking and introduced themselves. At some point, Archangel Michael told me that he would always be by my side and he was there to protect me. No more hurt. He said that I have been hurt so much in my life that my soul is so damaged that it doesn't exist. That is when Archangel Raphael told me to look at him. He said to me, "Alicia, this is your soul."

All I saw on him was holes everywhere! Holes beyond repair. He said these holes were my wounds from all the hurt and pain I had been enduring. It was time to heal!

"I will make you feel whole again and I will heal you. It will not happen immediately, but you will be whole again."

I hugged them both and cried. I cried to my heart's content. They consoled me and told me not to worry. They were gentle Giants. My dream ended and the first thing I did was Google these names and search more on Archangels. To my disbelief, I found that I had, had actual angels visit me. I read up on everything I could, even verses from the Holy Bible. They were real, as described. I gathered my thoughts and cried. I went to my prayer place and cried some more. I was so damaged by all my trauma and life's rollercoaster.

I didn't know who to tell, who would believe me if I had to say Archangel Michael and Raphael spoke to me. I kept it to myself. Years later, I shared it with three people that could relate and understood what I saw in my dream. Today, I share it with you. I always say "Have full faith in the one you believe in." Swami says, "Love all, Serve all."

COVID-19 stepped in with a loud bang which sent us all into a lockdown. Many lost income and family to the virus. Businesses closed down, which left huge numbers of unemployed. With Swami's grace, my husband and I were grateful to have been called back to work in May 2020. Retrenchments claimed many jobs in the company I worked for, which meant that those left behind had to do the work of three or more people for the same salary. I prayed for a sign and asked Swami to please show me a way out of this. A few weeks into being back at work, things started to change there and it became more demanding. As the employee, you just had to agree to everything. I am not that person! With all the unfairness and terrible management of this company, I put in my resignation with immediate effect. Yes, call me stupid because I need a job, income and the benefits, but I will not put myself at risk for greediness and for a company were employee wellbeing means nothing. My husband told me, "I'd rather have a stress free, happy wife than someone who is constantly unhappy."

With my husband's support, I left this demanding job amidst the pandemic, to be happy.

I resigned from my job in July 2020 and it was time to fly. A week before this decision, I had written "It's time to fly" in my journal, not knowing that a week later, it meant leaving my job. I know Swami had and has a plan for me. He will lead me. Swami has a plan for me and I trust him fully.

During the lockdown, I realized I don't need much. I questioned Swami so much and all I could feel was, "What are you short of?" And I always arrived at the same answer. Nothing. I have everything. I only need a small amount of money for my debit orders, I need my husband, I need my fur babies and I need Swami. I am not one for material things, I don't have any debt so I can live comfortably on money I receive from my investments. What more do I need? Nothing! Nothing at all. If I look at what I have gained, I have more time with my 2 fur babies, Kiara and Chloe, I have time to cook those beautiful meals I once cooked, I can rest, I can do my extra prayers and meditations every single morning without feeling guilty. I am happy and I am at peace!

You have no idea of the mind space I am in when I say I am at peace. I still get asked when I am going to start looking for a job. It is the least of my worries. Work is not everything. We spend our lives working and we never enjoy the joys of the life we are supposed to lead. We put 110% into things for another person's company. Why can we not direct that towards growing ourselves? I have worked hard for everything all my life. Lockdown has taught me to slow down and enjoy.

So, instead of asking me if I am looking for a job, rather ask me if I am happy!

I have come so far and I guess for the last lap of life, it's time to rest a little. I celebrate life more than ever and I welcome all the manifestations to come. Swami works in weird and wonderful ways.

I know this is the same belief that followers of other faiths have about their leaders. So many have tried to change my religious beliefs, as I have mentioned earlier, especially from Hinduism to another religion. They picked on my prayers, Gods and said my religion is the work of the devil. It saddened me because I may not pray to who you believe in but I know you trust in your supreme being. Just as I trust in my supreme being. I was taught to love all religions, to show the utmost respect to other religions and never to try to convert another person to my religion. Please stop trying to convert people. I feel that if you don't believe in the religion you are born into, go ahead and find one that you feel comfortable in, but don't force a person just because it has worked for you.

I have seen Swami's miracles, blessings and manifestations and his teachings are simple. I have been prayed for from different faiths and I am blessed for that, because at the end of it all, we all pray for peace, love and wellbeing. We pray to different Gods in different names and forms but with the same message.

Swami is my everything and he has never failed to show me his beautiful miracles. Swami caught me and held my hand and I never fell; I was uplifted by his spiritual bliss in the form of dreams, while I sat at his Divine Lotus feet. My beautiful life that I live, the reason for me being here today, is through Swami. All thanks and love to my Swami.

I stopped questioning Him as to why this and why that. I have accepted that he wants me to do His work. This, my story, became strength and motivation for many and I found my calling. My purpose for being alive is to save lives as I am living proof you can get through so much. With every step I took, I had Swami's full blessings. I have never visited Swami's ashram and I hope that one day I am graced to visit. Swami has come into my dream numerous times and he has asked, "When are you coming to visit the ashram?"
It is on my list to visit and I will soon, Swami.

So often, we lose faith in our religious beliefs because it takes too long to materialize into what we have prayed for. Time and patience are the key. I have seen it and I believe in prayers of all forms. Never lose faith in the one you have full faith in! From my experiences, dreams and messages of Swami, I could write another book. But I do know that I am here for a reason, a greater purpose, and Swami has blessed me with more than I could have ever imagined. It's at this point in my life that I don't ask Swami for anything, unless someone is sick and I need healing prayers to be sent out. This may sound weird, but I bless Swami because he has given me everything and I have nothing to ask for.

"I bless you Swami and thank you for everything you have given me in this life and more."

I ask Swami to bless people I come across. I say a silent prayer for people walking by, even my enemies are blessed with a prayer.
There have been numerous times I have had strangers come up to me and just start a conversation about their life and hardships. I am obviously blown away by the testimonies and truly amazed by their

strength, but more so that Swami has not only put this person in my path for that moment, but he has made me an instrument so that people can talk to me openly.

You know, before this book could get published, I went through so many channels and I didn't even understand why. I registered for a masterclass Webinar, to learn how to get my book out there and while the host was talking about "Marketing and Strategy", he mentioned so many things. With every word, I started to check these check boxes in my head and would you believe me if I said that everything was checked? I had gone through, so much, from TV and radio interviews, writing articles and columns, sharing my story on social media, creating a platform for Warriors to feel free to talk and be inspired to live. I felt it was just a maze, doing this and that, but everything that I had done, every single life lesson and person I met, led up to this moment.

It led me to the bigger picture of the final product of getting my book published.

I never questioned why, I just did it.

I am truly blessed to be able to do the work I do because of Swami. Love all Serve All. Bless you, Swami, always and forever, your devotee.

Om Sai Ram

REFLECTION

If the God's/Goddesses/Supreme beings up in the heavens don't pass judgement. Who are humans to find fault and judge? What if the aspect of "abnormal" is the normal and vice versa?

Where blue is actually red and red is actually yellow! What if this is a way to learn to love unconditionally regardless of race, religion, backgrounds, illnesses and most importantly not to judge. If we could master this concept to accept everyone as they are and try not to change them.

PART 3

17

REFLECTIONS

You now know the pain that I went through, saying goodbye to two innocent siblings who never got to venture into this world, and my parents, who I wish I had more time to get to know.

People ask,
"How have you managed to overcome all of this?"
Honestly, it's truly God's grace and my willingness to go on, to see a full life, from start to end. I turned this pain into something powerful and to prove a point to my family that I made it and I am not everything that they told me I am! And also, to show the many out there that, no matter what you are going through, it will pass. Rise and climb that ladder. Those failures? Use them as stepping stones to get to the top. Why not?

We should not let our failures bring us down. What have we learnt from that failure? There is always a lesson.

My will to fight another day will continue and I will stand strong. The stories and lessons learnt since the age of 12 led me to start writing this autobiography. I wish I had done it sooner, but the time and place have finally culminated in me completing this, in the year 2021.

My heart bleeds when I read this book over and over. It brings tears to my eyes and I can never imagine or see myself, or anyone going through this again. It is true it is real and raw.

I have been told that I am selfish. I am not selfish! If you have never wronged anyone or sinned, then you can judge me but if you haven't, I suggest you shut up.

I have grown to have next to no feelings towards those that have caused such pain while I was growing up and pray that they do see that they, too, are not perfect in many ways. I know a lot of family have not forgiven my parents or me for that matter. Or they have forgiven one, but not the other.

I know that many find it hard to forgive their loved ones for their suicide attempt and many other incidents. As I've grown older, I understand that my father did what he did because of my mother's affair and my mother died by my father's hands, which unfortunately took the lives of my siblings. Only years later, I have realized this event had so many aspects I could have spoken off but I chose to speak and spread the awareness of suicide. I am cutting away at sitting with silence and pain, cutting away the stigma that is so prevalent in our communities about suicide and mental illnesses. This book, my story, will open those doors and allow everyone to open up and reach out for help.

I have never opened up in so much detail before. And I guess it was time to show everything, that lies below the iceberg. People only saw the tip and what I've shared in my videos, articles and columns. It was time to speak up.

In my life, I have forgiven both my parents for this, as I need their souls to rest and find peace. Their journey to heaven awaits. More importantly, I have peace within me. You need to make peace. It is not easy, but you need to make peace and forgive.

I could not carry this anger for them in my heart, but forgiveness was not an immediate action. It took years to forgive.

I wish I could tell you all your grieving will go away, that the pain will stop. It does not.

I went through various stages of my grieving. Things that, at that point, I did not understand but now I do and I can place myself at healing and living till the end.

These stages of grief were:
- Denial
- Anger
- Coming to terms
- Making peace and forgiveness
- Healing
- Living till the end

My family's murder-suicide was obviously not something I could have prepared myself for. There was no way for me to know what my life would have in store for me. Suicide does come as a shock, and we never know how to react. That is why I look forward to each birthday. I welcome life and its curveballs.

I've handled natural deaths better than this murder-suicide.

There is a saying, "In time you heal."
Honestly speaking, I have learnt to live without them. I guess part of the healing is that I have made peace with my family's death. That heartache is still there, and it will never go away. I have accepted that they are no longer, and we will meet one day in the Heavens. I have learnt to live without them by my side, I have grown stronger emotionally and mentally that I am able to share my life's experiences and lessons to help those go on.

Those wounds of loss and grief are buried in me. I feel it every day without fail.

Create memories.
Memories are so powerful.
It's so important to create memories because that's a sign that we have lived. I promise you, I hold onto those great memories I had with my late family. Some days those are the things that get me through, that help me to push on. As much as I want to give up, I can hear my parents saying
"Don't give up!"

What I am trying to say is, you never get over loss of that loved one. It will hurt, and the days to come will make you strong. You will not forget them. Everything you do is a reminder of them.
We must go on, we must.

I wish that, as an adolescent, I had the support that was needed to deal with my trauma. It is so important to ask for help. It is so important to say that you are not ok. I should have done that too, and I didn't because I was scared. The times that I wanted to kill myself,

I only saw one way out, but there are always a million solutions. We need to understand that when we lose a loved one, it's not only one person that is affected, but many, and we all deal with it differently. Sometimes we need help.

I urge you to reach out. It is ok to not be ok! I still have my moments when my anxiety gets to me. My family's birthdays, their death anniversary, festive seasons, Mothers and Father's Day, still brings me to tears. And it is ok to feel this way. Adults made me feel useless and that by me living, I was taking up the oxygen they inhaled. I felt suffocated on so many occasions that it took a lot of positive self-talk to build me up again. I took up courses to encourage and uplift myself, I read books to understand positive self-talk, to affirm, to remind myself that I am a good person. I had to stand strong. It isn't easy to learn to be positive in every situation, we need to learn to lock out that negativity. All that hate talk and hitting myself in front of a mirror. I wish I could take it back and tell my younger-self;
"You are worth so much more, you are a beautiful, talented and intelligent being."

It hurt a lot when the people I loved, hurt me, but I also realized that it was not worth having such people in my life, if they did this. Likewise, they felt that I had hurt them and preferred to break ties with me. I won't be surprised if more ties are broken after this book has been read. Let them be, and you move on without them, just as they have moved on without you.

You are so much more. Look into that mirror and see that beautiful being standing there looking back at you.

I had to learn to love myself before loving the next. I can't be hating myself and telling another to love. You need to love you! That is why sharing my story and starting the group came in so late. I had to learn to heal myself in order to heal the next.

You do you, darling.

I am worth so much more. I realized this a bit too late, but I truly am worth a lot more than what people thought of me.

And so are you! You are such a Warrior and I need you to see that in you.

Below is a story about a carrot I shared on my group *Surviving Suicide: 05 July 2019*

A Carrot Story...

See, a few months ago at our clock station at work, I saw a little sprout. It baffled me. How did this thing start growing here?

As it grew, I figured it was a Carrot seedling!

My first instinct was to pull it out, take it home and look after it.

I tugged; it just wouldn't budge! It was so grounded.

I was off work for 1.5 weeks, and when I got back, the first thing I went to check on was the Carrot plant.

This plant didn't get watered daily neither did it get fertilizer.

I was amazed to see how beautiful and healthy it had grown.

It had healthy green leaves and it was pushing through, so any day now it would be ready to be harvested.

This Carrot plant had inspired me because...

How many times in life we are put into harsh environments?

How many times do we forget to take care of ourselves?

This plant survived, growing in a harsh environment.

No matter how hard or harsh your environment is, I want you to grow.

I want you to ground yourself and plant your roots deep.

I want you to Surface!

Don't forget who you are!

This Carrot nurtured itself, regardless of the environment it grew in.

It fought!

It chose life!

I know it's just a Carrot, but I'm proud of this being.

In your tough times, remember this Carrot story and push through!

Photo: The Carrot at my workplace

I look at everything and, yes, there was a difference in how I was brought up versus how my cousins were brought up by their biological parents. I know that everyone says that they love me, and they are always there for me, but to date I know that I am different and maybe it's just that we try to make up for the wrongs we have done to make the present and future correct. I don't see your children living the way I did.

I want to tell all of you who played a role in looking after me:
Many of you, and this goes to extended friends and family of ours, felt that I was ungrateful, and I did not say thank you for anything. I was and still am, forever grateful for everything that every person did for me.

Thank you for giving me a home and giving me whatever you could offer in my upbringing. Thank you for everything you have done, including the harshness and pain, because it made me stronger and I learnt to stand up for myself and learn to live without the toxic people and relationships.

Thank you for sending me to school and clothing me, thank you for allowing me to be part of your life and not allowing the system to claim me. Thank you for the hugs on my birthday, the shouting sessions for wrong doings, the well done in a good report, the congratulations, and the apologies. Thank you for straightening me up, thank you for giving me life again, thank you for all the knowledge, thank you for everything that I may have missed.

I am also sorry for not saying a proper goodbye the day I moved into my own place. You felt I should have said goodbye, but to me it sounds so final, and I didn't think I was leaving for good. After I moved out, my relationship with my adoptive mother was greater than ever, to a point of me looking forward to you asking what I would like to eat, having my favorite meal prepared when I visited, or you saw a nice dress and you bought it for me. We had even exchanged clothing and shoes because we were the same size. I wish that had happened earlier. I needed that when I moved to you, I needed that caring so much. I am sorry for hurting you and not being the child that everyone, including you, wished for. I am sorry that I was and still am, not perfect. I am sorry for not falling in love with a man that you find most acceptable. I am sorry that I married the man I love wholeheartedly and left my family for him, I am sorry that I fought back and said harsh words to you. I am sorry that I lived, while deep down you wished me dead instead of my siblings. I am sorry that seeing me alive caused you pain. I am sorry for whatever else you think needs apologies for.

As I move forward in my life, I want you to know that I am at peace with everything. I have forgiven everyone, but I will not forget. This book was started in 2006 as a reminder. I hold no grudge against anyone, not even my enemies. However, I will not associate myself and mend any toxic relationships. That stays there, and I do not wish to carry that forward. I know you don't invite me for your family get-togethers and that is ok, because I won't attend them either, for fear of being ridiculed. I have made peace with the fact that I do not fit into my own blood. I do love and miss you all. But you stay there, and I will stay here.

I do not wish for any family and friends who know any person in this book to change their relationship or attitude towards you. Please do not do that. This book was not written to declare war. These people have acted out of their best interest at that time, and they should not be treated differently after you read this book. I have written what I experienced as a child growing up. This is solely my story to tell. There are always two sides to a story so this is just my piece seen through the eyes of an orphan.

I wish you knew how much I love and loved each of you. This is where I will stop asking "What was so different about me?"
I am done and I am moving forward.

I have an amazing husband and his family supports my goals and loves me. Even though we have had our disagreements as a couple, my husband has grown and changed. He is a gem and that is why I am a spoilt brat! That was something someone once told me, that I am a spoilt brat, because my husband bought me a car. I guess my husband goes that extra mile because he sees through me. I am his wife and if he wants to buy me things, then let him.

I am happy, I am at peace and I am loving my life.
I can't believe that I lived through it all.
But I am here today to tell you, you can live through everything too. Suicide should not be the solution.

Quitting, well, I quit my studies because this is what I want to do not a BCom in Business Management Administration. And that is ok! But don't quit on you.

Survival mode was the only thing I knew until I started to really live, and I found that life is indeed beautiful. We need to love and find peace from within and, like I have said before, *love yourself first.* Fill your cup first, and when you are ready, pour some of that into someone else's cup.

I had no idea that one day I would tell you my life's story. Now imagine what your future may hold for you.

It never crossed my mind that this story, had I told it sooner, would save many lives and given hope to those on their last thread.

If you know of someone living with a mental illness, please assist them, even if you just hold space for that person. Take them seriously, do not disclose what they've told you in confidence to your neighbors and families. This is how we lose trust and hope of getting that person help.

Do not judge them. You have no idea what it took for them to just to say, "I need help."

As I said before,

I am not doing this for name and fame. I am on a mission in life to save a life. I hope my story has given you the inspiration and motivation to go on. Hang in there, because we will get through this.

Suicide is not the way to go.

Reach out for help. I am, and a million others are, ready and willing to listen to you.

You matter!

You are Loved!

Affirm that:
I am Love
I am Light
I am a Warrior

Someone told me that maybe this happened to me because I am the catalyst of change. It got me thinking and it actually made sense. This book is the change that needs to happen. This book is the catalyst of change!

REFLECTION

You can't start the next chapter in your life if you keep re-reading the last one. Maybe re-read it to remind you of how far you have come but don't go back to it.

18

CRUCIAL CONVERSATIONS

Remember the party for Ma, that time when Volcano Alicia decided that enough was enough? I had to eventually stand up to my elders. Something we need to learn in life. It doesn't mean that, because you are an elder, you are always right and that you will always have your way. This person had lost my respect for them a long time before this event, not because I felt better than them, but because I knew I was right and she was wrong, in this case. Swallow that bitter pill of truth, as I did. Names have been removed from this conversation to protect the identities of the people involved. The private investigator part was a white lie, but I did have all my father's original documents. I said it more to call the rat out.

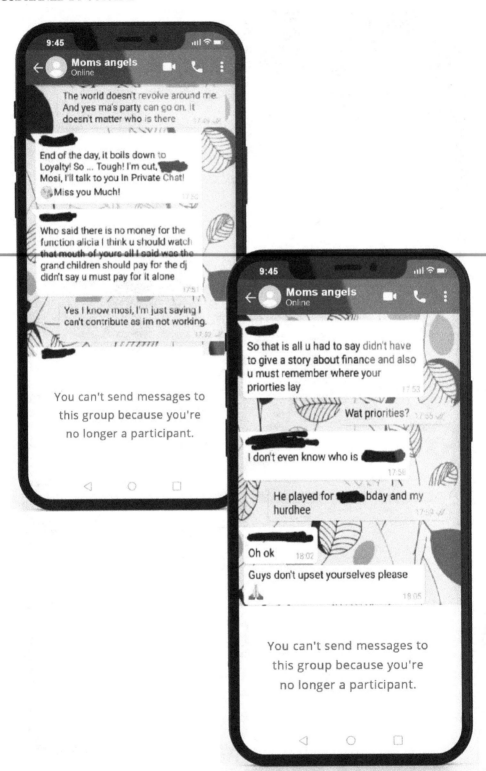

The first phone shows a conversation:

15:18
Everytime u open your mouth u create problems must let your inlaws know. If u can have your mother and siblings killed u capable of anything over and out u history in my books

19:19
U know wat u killed them

U knew mum was having an affair

Stop blaming me for their death

U knew everything

That's y u cant live with urself

They dead beacause of u

I got recordings and letters from police. Dad wasn't in debt like u lied about. Dad did it cause mum was having an affair and all of u knew except for me. So how can I kill my family if I was in jhb and the last call was to u. Stop playing the blame game God is going to punish u for all your wrong deeds.

The second phone shows:

19:26
Alicia I. Have all the evidence right here with me i will forward so why was the house auctioned

19:27
U are a murderer not me, u sent them to their grave. Plz do U have no papers i have all original work. My private investigator got the rest. So stop with ur lying

And making me a lier

Mum did have an affair she admitted it even wen we went to the medium in dbn wen i was with all of u

Stop lying

Type a message

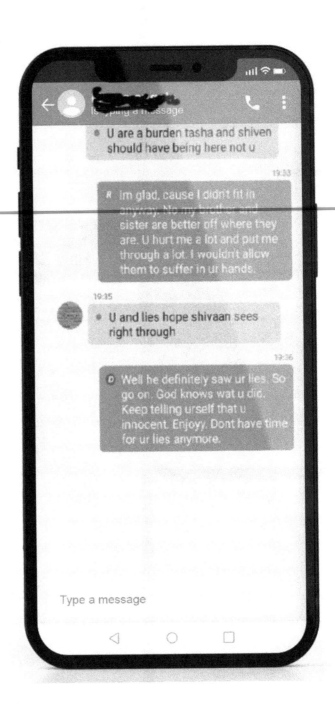

Hi hope u are well, just want to say that I was quiet for a few days cos I was and still is uncomfortable with the interview and the way you handled a specific issue, sorry but I need to be critical on this as you have on numerous occasions degraded and made assumptions on your Late mother, I do not interfere in your life, but belittling a woman that gave birth to you is not justifiable, from the little that I knew your mother I always admired her for her beauty, kindness and lovable nature. However I do not approve of her name being slandered on national TV apart from social media, I would be lying to you if I said that it was good cos families have actually shunned me on this, as I had advised them to watch it on ___ feeling proud to have you on the air. However this backfired from my side but I really needed to air it out. Please if I am wrong let me know as whatever has been done is done and it is really sad that your own moms name is being degraded, really sad Alicia 😊😊😊

This conversation was after I had done the TV interview and my adoptive parents and my adoptive father's family was offended by the way I had answered specific questions.

Hi
Thank you for bringing this up.
I did take note of everyone's silence
especially from my side of the family.
But this is not an assumption.
My mother did have an affair and my family
hid that from me.
Everyone can be upset with me for saying
so. Like I had said in the interview if I was not
there to see or hear who am I to judge my
dad for his Suicide or my mum's affair if she
did.
I forgave them.
A school boy came forward a few years ago.
He confessed due to his conscience
worrying him that he could not stop   and
my mother's relationship.
They tried and eventually they told my father.
So if my family wants me hide like they've
hidden alot of things from me then let it be.
I am not at all embarrassed about my
mother even if she did have an affair she
found love. Love that maybe her arranged
marriage never gave her.
I think my family knew of my mother and

But that's just my side of the story.
I've had not only students but the detectives
that were there that day tell me things since
I've opened Surviving Suicide.
Lies or not
Truth or not
But I'm tired of just being hush about what
happened   11:58

Type a message

This interview was not live, it was a pre-recorded video that I did at home. The questions were sent to me and I had to answer them. Some people felt I lied because "I couldn't look the camera in the eye." Well, I had to turn away to read the questions. It's scary how people perceive things and reality. The same goes with everything else that is said from the Facebook post. Clearly, you have no idea why I run Surviving Suicide and the work that I do. It's not for name and fame but for saving lives, for Warriors out there to reach out and talk about what they are going through. With all these messages I am not crying wolf or playing the victim. Everyone sees things differently. And from my view, I had grown up around people like this then it makes me wonder. Go in peace, wherever you are. It's one of the ties that I will not go back to.

From ▓▓▓ side of the family, we have not interfered in you life, infact we showed you a lot of love.

14w

Alicia Ramdharee
▓▓▓▓▓▓▓▓▓with all due respect please comment on the group or on my fb page this is someone elses post

14w   Like   Reply

Type a comment

dont seem capable of that yet. You fight with your mothers family, yet they too lost a sister and a daughter, they too loved her, yet you are so nasty to them. National TV, social media, all of it, all your efforts are a waste of time, if you cannot and will not acknowledge the love that you really had. Sooner or later, you will be found out. Its sad, so sad, that you go on TV and paint such a story about yourself to the world. Tell the world how you survived with the love you had from K███ and ████, whom you could never acknowledge as your parents, about the love you had from ████ and S████ who consider you to be there own flesh and blood sister, from the rest of your family who showed you love in some way or the other. You were never left to roam the streets as an orphaned child often is, or put into an institution. You were so loved and well taken care of. Your mum and dad would rest in peace knowing you were in good hands...but thats not what you felt...Im afraid more and more people have and will see through you and its not about haters out there, its about the Truth, Love and Peace. Learn well if you can. It will help you teach your own children one day. God bless you.

2m   Like   Reply

████████

no need for respect Alicia, you dont know the meaning of that word. My apologies to that someone else, im not a good face book user, however, this was my way of reaching out to Alicia. I too loved her so much, no i dont know what i feel. ████ is my brother. I love him and i cant bear to see his pain.

Just now   Like   Reply

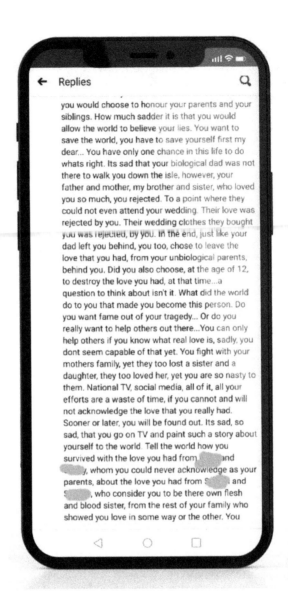

In all of these conversations I never held or had any hard feelings towards anyone, they all have acted in a way they felt was and is right. So, I let them be. I am at peace within me, and I am done arguing and trying to prove anything to everyone. I do sleep peacefully at night. I forgave and forgive but I will not forget. Bless you all and may you live a peaceful life.

REFLECTION

The proof is always in the pudding. When you are told things so often, you tend to believe them. Sometimes we need proof to remind us that we are NOT what they say we are! And that they don't know the real you.

A quote I came across… "People may destroy your image, stain your personality but they can't take away your good deeds… because no matter how they describe you, you will still be admired by those who really know you better."

Today I feel better,

Today I feel better because as much as I try to fit in with family "I
never will",

I have always been the black sheep, the runt of the lot, the rule
breaker, the disappointment, the burden, the not-so-perfect child.

I have a heart of gold.

I carry light within me so bright it blinds my scars and leads the way
for others.

Today I feel better because those that have not mended their ways
have been punished.

Today I feel better because I will not be hurt again.

Today I feel better because I stand from my hill watching.

Today I feel better because I have come to terms that I will never be
accepted into the pack called "family"

Today I celebrate because I no longer hurt.

Alicia 'Sewdass' Ramdharee

About The Author

Alicia "Sewdass" Ramdharee is a speaker and the founder of a Suicide Awareness support group-aimed at giving hope, inspiration, and motivation to those left with the burden of dealing with suicide.

This passion has led to her resigning from her corporate admin role to pursue the purpose of creating awareness about suicide and mental health.

Following her move from Durban to Johannesburg at 12 years old, due to the tragic loss of her family, Alicia now resides in Rustenburg with her high school sweetheart and now husband, Schivan.

When not raising the alarm on suicide and its effects, she enjoys travelling and experiencing exotic places and foods around the world.

Her mission in life is to save a life, even if it is just one life at a time.

Printed in the USA
CPSIA information can be obtained
at www.ICGtesting.com
LVHW040320220923
758957LV00020B/124